MW01180706

# LIFEYOGA MANIFESTO

## Insideout Transformations

*A Guided Journey Through The Transformative Process*

AUTHOR | LYNNE GARDNER

LIFEYOGA, LLC
Lynne@lifeyogaworld.com

Developed by Lynne Gardner
© LifeYoga
All rights reserved

© Artwork by Beau Kissler
© Cover Design/Layout , by Matt Abron

First Edition, June 2013
P.O. BOX 1416 Carnelian Bay, Ca 96140

GARDNER, LYNNE
 LifeYoga Manifesto 2013
1st ed.
ISBN - 13: 9781494363758

# FORWARD

It is with the deepest gratitude for my students, clients, family, and all inquisitive humans being that I offer the words and ideas contained in this book. Like any form of human expression, these pages are not only a means to communicate knowledge and ideas; they are a direct reflection of the source. The stories, information, insights, and theories herein are a direct result of my life journey and personal transformation. As I always stress to my students and clients the importance of understanding the origin and source from which information is obtained; I feel that is necessary to offer the reader some insight into my own life and experiences.

As a child, I was gifted with the challenge of severe scoliosis; a potentially disabling condition which forced me to acknowledge and utilize the transformative power of my soulful intention, breath, and nervous system. The gift of my battle with this disability offered me an amazing insight to transformative process. At a very young age, I was forced to deal with the frightening reality that my physical body was literally growing and spiraling out of control. Deep down inside I knew I must find a way to transform my spine and body lest I become physically incapacitated and disfigured; or worse yet, physically immobilized by a surgeon.

My childhood intuition and determination led me to discover a way of being, a process by which I could transform my physical body with the sheer will of my soulful intention and breath. Although, at the time, I was quite cognitively unaware of exactly how I was creating this transformation in my body and life, I soulfully knew and physically felt that I possessed the power within my being to alter my skeletal structure; and so… I did. Despite the fact that I spent many years of my childhood in full body braces, my practice of what is now defined as the LIFEYOGA Breath and Energy Transfer System not only kept me from potential crippling and the experience of full spinal fusion at the age of fourteen; it allowed me to drastically alter the condition of my disability to the extent that I was able to be a competitive gymnast and later on, and accomplished dancer.

Throughout the following years, in the attempt to better understand my own transformative life path and empower others with this knowledge, I studied and searched for a succinct and meaningful explanation of this empowering process of transformative choice. Thankfully, I had the good fortune to engage with many great teachers and brilliant minds; from quantum physicists, anatomists, and neurologists, to yogis, Buddhists, philosophers, and eastern and western medical doctors. This eclectic background of science and spirituality has led me to a means of didactic explanation of transformative process in the human condition. This explanation is held within these pages.

Over the years, as a result of my practice and teachings in yoga and yoga therapy, I have had the opportunity to observe and facilitate this transformative process in countless bodies and lives. I have found that before the student or client can grasp and utilize the mechanics and intricacies of the Breath and Energy Transfer Process, he or she must first understand how the process works, and the philosophies and reasoning behind it. This is the purpose of this book: to discover why and how we can be in transformative choice.

This work is not intended to be an answer or a "how to" manual, but a question and guided insight into the process of transformative self- discovery, transformative choice, and empowerment. It is meant to be, in itself, an exploration, a transformative journey and basis for the practice of LIFEYOGA. Any assumptions or intricacies of factual and scientific knowledge herein, while entirely valid, have not been discussed or referenced in great detail, as this book is intended to be an accessible experiential short read rather than a lengthy textbook. Complete factual intricacies, detailed explanations, and references have been saved for longer future works.

# Table of Contents

CHAPTER ONE

**Reason**

PAGE 7

CHAPTER TWO

**The Question**

PAGE 13

CHAPTER THREE

**Realities Of The Universe**

PAGE 17

CHAPTER FOUR

**Realities Of Being Human**

PAGE 21

CHAPTER FIVE

**Expansion**

PAGE 25

CHAPTER SIX

**Intention**

PAGE 43

CHAPTER SEVEN

**Manifestation**

PAGE 61

CHAPTER EIGHT

**Energy**

PAGE 85

CHAPTER NINE

**Being**

PAGE 113

CHAPTER TEN

**Wheel Of Life**

PAGE 137

CHAPTER ELEVEN

**If**

PAGE 157

# Reason

*"Mama Ant carried her egg on her back to the cool shade beneath the great grey sky. She nestled it carefully in the soft jungle of grass next to the great grey pillar of Eleph-Ant. She waited."*

When I close my eyes, I can still feel that day. I can smell the fear and anticipation of my seemingly shadowed unknown. I bathed in my desire to own it, to pass through it with dignity, unscathed. The cold air nipped at my freshly showered skin as moisture crept gingerly out of the weathered tiles in a translucent rain that caused my flesh to slightly shiver. Proudly, I stood up to my reflection in the cloudy glass. It stared boldly back at me as if to trick me, reminding me that *I* was, that *I* existed in his shell of a body; a container for my sensation, movement, and thoughts that *they* described as irreparably damaged and destined for destruction.

Their voices began closing in, echoing their perceived reality from the expanding bathroom walls. "She will feel pain. She may cease to walk. She will slowly morph into an abomination of herself... grow and expand helplessly into a compressed and lesser body."

My ears rang, collapsing into my head. My skin crawled. Their words cut at my soul; a premonition of the steely knives *they* would use to sever my precious flesh and fix my spine of reality to suit their perception and awareness. My pulse raced. " How could *they*? How could *they* know my intention or my path by a simple snapshot of my container, a less than a second's perception through their monsters' eye? Did *they* see me, or simply my reflection through their reality? "

I stared blindly into the misty glass. The body that looked back at me was just a body, a mass of bones, nerves, and tissue. And yet, this was my body. *I* could feel it. *I* breathed in it, through it, and around it. *I* breathed. *They* did not breathe for me, but only for themselves. *I* was. I breathed and breathed.

And the longer I breathed, the longer I felt, I began to notice the body before me as a gently pulsating mass; continually opening out of itself into the misty air. I became transfixed by the sound and sensation of my own breath and the expansion of my own *being*... *my self* moving in, through, and out of myself. Suddenly, *I* had no boundaries. I was awed and amazed at the power and grandeur of my own soul as it grew out of my body. In that moment of my ten years, I discovered that *I* created my own reality, my own *being*. My practice had begun.

The mist began to clear. *They* became simply a complication of my mind's eye perception. The enclosing walls receded as my body began to warm and clear the space. I began to soulfully expand from the inside out, transforming the reality of my "damaged container".

I inhaled, opening so much space in my center that I felt my skin and mind on the brink of explosion. I exhaled, compassionately releasing all that did not serve my soulful intention. I felt the power of my will engage at the base of my belly. It surged and manifested my intention down through the bones of my feet, rooting me into the earth with such a force that the resulting energy ricocheted back up through my center, pulling and lengthening the spine of my *being* up towards the endless sky. In a split second of perception, I was aware that my structure had changed. I expanded into and out of the moment. I inhaled. I exhaled. I manifested the energy of my intention into *being*. My yoga practice began.

And so I practiced every day, fresh from the shower in a misty bathroom; just me, my breath, my mind, soul and body, light and heavy with intention. I focused, I believed. The more I practiced, the more I experienced the subtleties of my bones, tissues, and nerves, the nuances of my mind. I transformed them with my soulful will. And eventually, as it does, my path led me back to *them.*

I felt a calm determination as *they* led me to stand before their monster of judgment, the x-ray machine *they* had chosen to dictate my destiny. The monster stared at me, fixated on my container. I smiled back at the helpless metallic beast that had once frightened me to tears.

Primed for the attack, I found myself deep in the love of my yoga.  I inhaled. I exhaled. *I* shined my soul through my container into its steely eyes until it was forced to blink and collapse a snapshot of the moment.

Their monsters' perception stared back at them. At first, *they* did not believe it….whatever *it* was.  At thirteen years old, I had changed their reality.

They sent me back to the judgmental beast for quite a few years to make sure that I was not a mere misperception of their monsters' eyes. Eventually, for lack of a better explanation, *they* chalked it all up to the fact that I had just "grown out of it".  I smiled up at them, humbled, now understanding that their reality was really mine.  Trembling, I stood a few inches taller in the old comfort of my new found spine and body, dumbfounded by the awareness and responsibility that the simple expansion of my soul's intention, my manifestation, *my being,* had altered *their* perception.  I grew beyond myself.

And as I grew into and out of the following moments and years, I found myself constantly searching for an explanation of this expansion and collapse of the soulful universe.  I studied the sciences, quantum physics, anatomy and physiology, kinesiology.  I studied and practiced music, dance, and the arts; all forms of intangible expression.  I read the books of the great philosophers; Plato, Nietzsche, Derrida, Merlot Ponti. I watched the world…business, politics, and culture.

Finally, I studied "yoga proper": the traditions, the various schools, the asana, the pranayamas and the affiliated philosophies and religions.

Yoga: The yoking of the soul with the self, the yoking of the soulful self with other, the yoking of the soul with higher collective consciousness.

Yoga: Quantum physics and spirituality; Expansion, Intention, Manifestation of Energy into *Being*.

Yoga: The soulful passion of the arts, transformation through the human body, the philosopher's answer and question in simultaneity.

Yoga: Religion undefined and unified.

And so I began to *be* in the realization that the answers that I had been searching for were ever opening into the questions themselves. My perceptions were and are merely an x-ray of consciousness, a snapshot of my momentary collapse into an ever-expanding collective reality. The practice of yoga was simply my *being* in awareness of my own expansion and collapse into that ever -changing collective consciousness. When *being* in this awareness, I had the soulful power to choose; to facilitate change in my physical body, my thoughts, my *being*. And if I had this power, so did *they*.

So it was that I discovered that *they* too, were searching. Eventually, they asked me to teach them this practice of yoga. I smiled up at them, humbled.

As a human *being* at practice, I did my best to teach them. I answered their detailed questions with my perceptions of breath, energy, asana, kinesiology, history, and philosophy. I did my best to facilitate their process of practice. I showed them my x-rays, and encouraged them to take their own. I watched them fill their minds and bodies with their own perceptions of the knowledge and tools that I gave them. And yet all the while, despite the apparent perceptive complexities, the practice and the teaching of this phenomenon called yoga was, and is, simply the Expansion, Intention, Manifestation of Energy into *Being*. How does one teach another how to *be* in *being*? I became the student.

As I continue to practice and teach, I now realize that *I am*, that *we are* all, like it or not, aware or unaware, students and teachers of Expansion, Intention, Manifestation of Energy into *Being*. By simply *being*, we are all in the yoga, however present. *We are* the yoga. Through our practice, and the willingness to *be in awareness* with the yoga that *we are*; our thoughts, our intentions, and our actions not only constantly transform and enhance our own lives, they transform our world as we know it. *I* and *we* create *it*. The practice of yoga is the practice of *being* the awareness of that which is *being*… life. LIFEYOGA: the practice of *being* in life.

The following is a moments' glance into the possibilities of the many ways to be *being* in life, in LIFEYOGA. It is not intended to be *the* answer. It is not intended to be *an* answer, rather; a tool; a means by which to expand into and out of the questions of the soul, the body, and the mind as we breathe through the moments of instantaneous transformation and create the infinite realities of our world.

# The Question

*"Baby ant lay curled up, safe and snug in his egg.*
*Quite suddenly, in a moment or a year, miraculously he awoke.*
*He shifted and stretched his newfound antennae.*

*Mama Ant felt her egg wiggle and wondered."*

As humans *being*, we have known for years through the experiences of religion, spirituality, meditation and yogic practices, that we are somehow connected to the power of the universe, however defined. We have understood for quite some time that we can move the breath and intentions through the body and mind in a way that leads us closer to the feeling of that universal power. Even though most of us have all felt or experienced" that connection" at some point; until recently, we haven't really had any scientific proof of the process.

Thanks to the rise of the science of quantum physics and expansion theory in recent years, we are now able to better understand the nature of the universe as it exists in both spirituality and in the reality of the physical world.   Spirituality, whether it is quantified in Buddhism, Taoism, Christianity, any other religious affiliation, or simply "nothingness" now has actual physical, scientific, real live proof of existence. *Something*, some causal energy exists within us and within the physical world. This causal energy, however we define It; as God, collective consciousness, energetic matter… whatever It is; is constantly creating and transforming the universe. Through science, we know that this causal energy of our world is constantly expanding and collapsing into our perceived reality.

Through the work of quantum physics, we now understand that as part of this energy, however defined; we too are in a constant state of expansion and collapse. The textbook definition of being alive is "being in a state of constant instantaneous transformation." By simply *being* we constantly transform fabric of ourselves and our universe.

The brilliance of sub atomic experiments such as "Schrodinger's Cat" has allowed us to discover that our intentions; our conscious and sub conscious feeling and knowing are causal. With our soul felt thoughts and intentions, the energy of our *being*, we collapse and cause our transformations, our perceived realities, both individually and collectively. We, through the energy of our soulful intentions and *being*, decide what transformation is occurring.

This means you are actually creating yourself, your own instantaneous transformations every second, every breath from the inside out. You may not be aware of the transformation you are creating, but you are creating it. Aware or unaware, every less than a second you decide the physical body of *you*, and the reality you that you experience.

Now the power of this knowledge is incredible, so incredible that we have just begun to learn about and explain it in a way that allows us to access it. While great books and movies such as "The Self Aware Universe", "What the Bleep" and "The Secret" have made this information available to the masses; most humans, even those who follow a path of self- discovery still do not fully understand how to access and utilize this information in practical terms. The process of *how* we choose, manifest, and collapse our own reality remains an open question.

How do we in awareness actually make our chosen soulful intention, breath, and being causal?

How do we choose our intentions?

As humans being, how do we transfer this knowledge and causal energy through the systems of our human body meat-suit, and make it our reality?

And when through this soulful intention we do actually move through ourselves in awareness and be and create our own realities; how do we deal with the self -responsibility and accountability of that?

How do we use this soulful causal power?

How do we choose to transform ourselves, our reality, our world?

The following is an experiential process: a journey through the "LIFEYOGA Wheel of Life": Expansion, Intention, Manifestation, Energy, and *Being*. As you travel through the world of these words you will gain insight into the nature of transformation itself, the nature of the universe as it is constantly transforming, and the nature of you as you exist and transform in this transformative universe. You will find in these pages a foundation, a basis of eclectic knowledge; solid roots that allow you to travel through and connect with the physical and spiritual worlds. Through an in depth adventure into your breath and being, you will discover how you can use the tools of your soulful intention, your breath, physical body, nervous system and perceptive senses to identify and break through any conscious or sub conscious barriers that inhibit transformative power. You will bask in the possibility and truth of *being* in a way that manifests your soulfully desired intention as transformative reality.

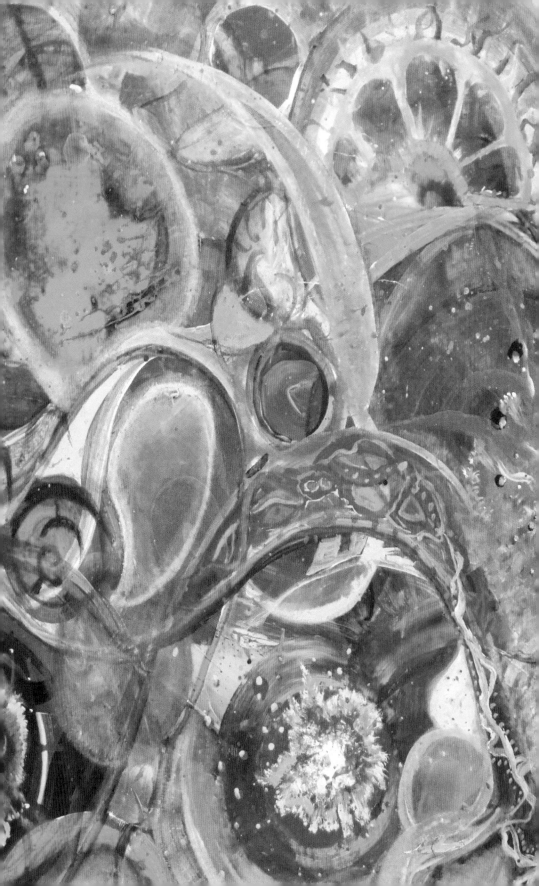

# **3**

# **Realities Of The Universe**

*" 'Maaaaaaama!' cried Baby Ant as he hatched from his egg.*
*'The world is getting bigger and bigger!' "*

Although we are constantly finding new, changing, and more in depth information about our universe, both modern science and yogic experiences have proven certain things about the physical world to be true. These truths act as a basis of our understanding of how the world's energies really work, and allow us to gain insight into how humans *being* actually fit into the process of the physical world. A true understanding of the parameters of our environment and the transformative possibilities that lie within are key to unlocking our transformative potentials. Because most humans *being* are not quantum physicists, Buddhist monks, or expansion theory experts, the following ideas, although quite complex in nature, have been as simplified as possible. Here are some basic realities to ponder and use as a framework as we move through the journey. Keep in mind, of course, that ultimately our intentions, perceptions, and *being* create these realities. They are expandable and subject to change.

1. The universe is made up of energy. As we know from Newtonian physics, "Energy is neither created nor destroyed. Energy IS. It simply changes form.

2. The universe and everything is it is in constant instantaneous expansion, collapse, and transformation.

3. All aspects of the expanding universe are intertwined, interrelated, and causal of each other.

4. The only constant is change.

5. Energetically speaking, the entire universe expands from the inside out. As humans *being*, our perceptive reality is created by the constant instantaneous collapse of this expansion.

6. "Energy", whether defined as God, collective consciousness, or simply "cosmic soup that is", is recreated and released in this constant instantaneous transformative process.

7. Human feelings and subconscious and sometimes conscious absolute knowing, both individual and collective, cause the collapse in the universe that creates our perceived reality.

# **Realities Of Being Human**

*" 'Maaaama' exclaimed Baby Ant as he balanced on four legs and wrapped his antennae into a trunk.*
*'Look at me! I'm an Eleph-Ant!'*

*'Silly Baby,' giggled his Mama.*
*'Don't you know you are an ant?' "*

Before we can discuss and explore the mechanics and principles that bring our soulful intentions to perceived realities, we must first understand a bit about what it means to be a human *being* in this endless sea of transformative possibility. We are alive in the physical world and having this discussion because we exist in human bodies. Here we are on this earth just hanging out; expanding within the realms of our human bodies and perceptive capabilities pretty much as souls   and energy in a meat-suit. We need to comprehend at some level the perceptive parameters and conditions of *being* in our bodies, so that we have a clue of how we move casual transformative energy in and through them. While these human realities remain expandable as we grow and break through perceptive barriers; these basic principles of humans *being* provide a tangible framework for the transformative process. Keep them in mind as we journey ahead.

1. As a part of the constantly transforming universe, you/we are in constant instantaneous transformation.

2. You are alive because you breathe. The breath is what links the trans-

formative possibilities of the universe to you. The act of breathing links the soul to the human body, soulful intention to the physical world.

3. Your breath controls your nervous system which controls everything you think, do, experience and perceive.

4. Everything that you think, do, or experience, affects your nervous system, which affects your breathing patterns and how you feel.

5. Feelings, subconscious / sometimes conscious "knowing" are ultimately causal…not cognitive thoughts or plans.

6. You can only *be* where and what you are.

7. You can only transform from where and what you *are*.

8. You can only perceive from who and how you are *being*.

9. Your *being* and perception of it, determines your transformative access.

10. How you are *being* is causal. *Being* chooses the transformation you are experiencing and the reality you are creating.

# Expansion

*" 'What is the sky?' asked Baby Ant.*
*'Just know that the sky I always grey' , answered Mama Ant*
*'Is it big?' asked Baby Ant*
*'It is grey,' sighed Mama Ant*
*'Mamaaaaa!' screeched Baby Ant,*
*'Haven't you ever been to the top of the Eleph-Ant?' "*

Just imagine the smallest particle, the tiniest speck you can see through your mind's eye. Then notice that particle expanding into two particles. Those two specks expand into four, to eight, to sixteen and so on. They expand until your world becomes filled with endless tiny particles that constantly expand, collapse, transform, and multiply.

Begin to feel this sea of incomprehensibly small particles moving through the sky, the trees, your chair, your breath; until the entire universe, including you is just a mass of expanding, collapsing, transforming specks that are endlessly intertwined.

Then know that every single little speck is a possibility, less than an instant of something that could happen or be.

This is the nature of our expansive universe, the transformative fabric that weaves our world, us, and our reality. Some call it "God". Some call it "Science". Some may name it "Collective Consciousness" or "Cosmic Soup". However defined, why or how, we know "it" is the infinite causal power of the universe, the great endless sea of possibilities from which we create and transform our perceived realities. From this happening, we happen, and are happening.

# Desiree

Desiree knew that she could fly. At age two and a half, she stood proudly on the heights of the coffee table; fairy wings perfectly positioned on her back, and screamed excitedly, "Look Daddy! I can fly!"

She took in a deep breath, and exhaled as she released herself up into the great expanse of the living room sky. For less than a second, she was suspended there in space, glittering wings fluttering as her two-year-old limbs flailed about in midair.

Plump! Her flying fairy hit the floor with a bump and she looked up with blissful radiant eyes and giggled excitedly,

"Did you see it? Did you see it? I can fly!"

"Great flying there Desiree," said Daddy, "I've always known you could fly!"

"Thanks Daddy," she replied. "I still need to practice my landing!"

The visiting neighbor, quite concerned, looked over at Daddy and asked, "Do you think its right to tell here that she *really can* fly?"

"She is *really* flying" he replied. "Why would I tell her that she isn't?"

At age four, Desiree was frustrated. She tugged at her worn wings. Flying just didn't feel like it used to feel. After all, she wasn't a real fairy! She wasn't Tinkerbelle! She stood stubbornly on the coffee table launching pad, held her breath, and forced her growing bones to fly into space. It was no use! She couldn't stay in the air no matter how hard she flitted or fluttered. In less than a second she landed solidly on her feet, reality weighing her down.

"Mama…"she whined. "I keep trying to fly but it just isn't working."

"You just keep practicing," said Mama. "I'm sure you'll figure it out!You certainly are landing well!"

Desiree sighed. "I wish I were a *real* fairy."

A determined young child who innately questioned the possibility of everything, Desiree continued to practice flying from the coffee table until the frustration of it moved her to tears.

"How would she ever be able to fly like a *real* fairy if she couldn't even fly off the coffee table?"

Stubbornly, she jumped and jumped again, but to no avail. Eventually exhausted by her own forceful efforts, she cried until the frustration passed and the tension of her *being* released. She lay spread eagle on the living room floor, stared up at the expanse of ceiling sky, sighed and wondered.

"What if there was another way to fly? What if she didn't really need to fly from the coffee table? What if she could fly from something else or in some other way? What if she didn't need to be a *real* fairy at all?"

Despite the frustration that she was a human *being* and not a *real* fairy, the moment Desiree released from holding her perceptive reality, she opened herself up to embrace and expand into the endless possibilities of flight. Once again she soulfully knew that "flying" was possible. Her physical body still grew heavier every moment, yet deep within her *being* she knew what it felt like to fly, and thus she constantly expanded her reality to accommodate flight. She was too big now to fly from the coffee table, so she simply began to fly off of ski jumps and diving boards.

At the ripe old age of almost six, Desiree is planning her fairy birthday party celebration. She wants to share the feeling of flight with her party guests, and she is devising ways for her fairy friends to fly at her celebratory gathering. Just yesterday she decided that airplanes might be a bit much for this year's party, but she is now expanding into the possibilities of swings, hammocks, parachutes, and trampolines. As she expands the reality of her own world, she creates the possibility for others to fly. Maybe she is a *real fairy* after all.

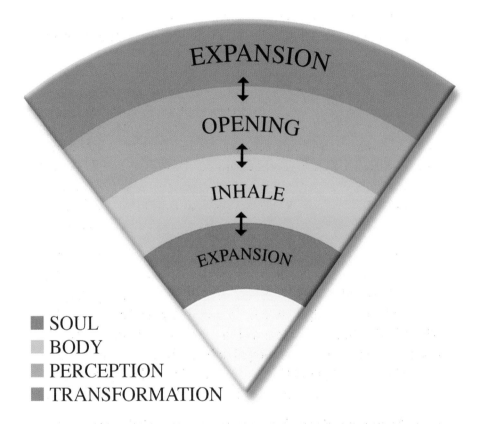

SOUL
BODY
PERCEPTION
TRANSFORMATION

# The Soul

The soul is the link between the fascia of the universe and our physical reality.  Because we exist in and are part of the sea of endless possibilities and transformative power; as humans being, by nature, we crave expansive thought and life experiences. We crave transformation. We are soulfully tied to it. We *are* it. In fact that feeling, that sub-conscious knowing, the sense of passion, soulful sense of self, is the causal force of all our transformation, whether we are aware of it or not.

Our soulful ability connect with and to *be* in this universal expansion; how much we truly know and feel is possible for us in the sea of possibility dictates our ability to access transformative change.

If we feel it is possible, it *is*.

If we can allow ourselves to move through the limitations of our human condition and nervous system, and literally *feel* and *be* open in the expanding universal energies, the transformative possibilities are endless. We simply must access them.

If our feelings of expansion are limited; consciously or subconsciously by our life experience and human conditions, (breath, nervous system, holding patterns and perceptions) our access to sea of possibility is limited. Transformative possibility and choice are compromised.

As our root of transformative possibility, expansion in the soulful sense,  however great or limited, dictates what is possible in the physical body and the physical world. However we open ourselves in soulful expansion chooses the possibilities from which we create our *being* and reality.

*So take a moment or a year to be in the soulful sense of your expansive transformative possibility.*

How much access do you feel that you have to the infinite sea of possibilities?

Do you soulfully know that anything is possible?

Does your mind or physical sensation kick in and limit the feeling of your soulful expansion and power?

Do you think first and feel later, or does your soulful awareness initiate your thoughts?

Do you experience difficulty with change?

What does expansion feel like? Space? Freedom? Fear?

# The Body

As humans *being*, we are alive because we breathe. The breath is what connects our soulful sense with the physical body and the physical world. The breath is what allows us to *be*; to live, think, create, manifest, and perceive in our physical reality. Manifestation of the expansive transformative power of the soul out into the physical world is entirely dependant on every inhale and exhale we experience.

Expansion in the physical body correlates directly to inhalation. As we breathe in and expand our lungs, not only do we take in oxygen and literally feed the body with universal energy; we expand and open the nervous system. As we feel the opening of the lungs and the associated tissues and fascias, the nervous system perceives space, safety, and possibility to create change. The nervous system controls everything we think, do, imagine and perceive; thus expansion in the nervous system is crucial in the transformative process.

A deep breath, an open nervous system allows the expansive transformative power of the soulful sense to enter the physical body and manifest change in the body and physical world. As we indulge in a deep inhale, the fascia of the body surrounding both the skeletal and organ systems literally opens and creates space in the tissues and neurological systems. This allows the subsequent exhale to release and transfer energy through open and receptive neurological pathways, tissues, and skeletal muscular systems.

Conversely, closed, restricted, held or shallow inhalation minimizes possibility in the nervous system. As we hold in inhalation, the fibers of our tissues hold, and the nervous system subconsciously/ sometimes consciously perceives lack of space, limited possibility, and often fear. This stifles soulful transformative power in the physical body and physical world. Literally, soulfully and neurologically, we are only as open to possibility for change and transformation as our inhalation is expansive.

Our life experiences and physical state of the body often affect our abilities to engage in full inhalation. If we are not breathing in fully and freely due to physical stress, emotional stress, neurological patterning, or trauma, we have diminished soulful access and neurological possibilities for change. We then "breathe smaller", feel smaller, and literally become smaller in our respiratory capacity. This cycle consciously and subconsciously feeds upon itself, causing further difficulty in accessing transformative expansion.

Sometimes, expansion itself simply becomes "too much". Because we exist as souls in human meat-suits, we can take in only as much expansive possibility as we have space to process in the physical body and nervous system. Over stimulation of our human *being*, either emotionally, mentally or physically can often cause us to "hold our breath" as a defense mechanism for taking in any more information or stimuli. We literally hold our breath to close our nervous system. While this human condition prevents us from spontaneously combusting with infinite possibility and overstimulation of our neurological systems, this "safety mechanism" of limited expansive intake can often become a regular inhalation pattern that subconsciously denies access to transformative power.

Our ability to *be* in expansive inhalation is dependant upon our ability to fully exhale and release the nervous system. If exhalation is compromised, we literally hold onto undesired toxins and holding patterns in the neurological system. This leaves little space for subsequent full inhalation, and therefore compromises our ability to experience full expansive transformative power.

Fortunately, the mechanism of the breath is both conscious and sub conscious. As humans *being*, we can, in any given instant consciously decide to expand into a deep breath, release in exhalation, and allow ourselves to open to the possibilities of soulful intention, and physical and neurological transformation.

*So take a moment or a year and notice how you inhale.*

Is it full and sumptuous?

Does it feel expansive?

Can you take breath into your belly, your ribs, your chest?

Does your inhale move up and down, or is it multi-directional?

Do you hold your breath when you are concentrating, speaking, or stressed?

How much expansion do you allow to enter your physical body?

Do you experience asthma or respiratory conditions?

Do you experience anxiety disorder or depression?

Do you experience poor balance or coordination?

Do you effort in movement?

# Perception

Expansive transformative possibility moves from the soul through the breath and nervous system, and eventually to the perceptive sense, the conscious and subconscious mind. The perceptive sense subconsciously and sometimes consciously tells us what happened in that last breath or split second of transformation, and then decides for us what is possible in the next moment or year. However we move soulful expansion through the breath and nervous system determines our perception of expansive possibility. If we soulfully feel expansion and experience full inhalation, we feel and perceive expansive possibility.

As we know from quantum physics and Buddhism, it is the soulful sense and the subconscious / sometimes conscious knowing in our *being* that actually create change and collapse soulful intention into reality. Conscious or subconscious, it is the feeling in our *being* that is causal. Our perceptive sense subconsciously decides how we are feeling and *being* through the tools of the breath and nervous system. The way in which our breath triggers subconscious perception is most often dictating our conscious sense of expansive possibility, and thus dictating the expanse of our transformative power.

As humans *being*, we need the perceptive sense to navigate in the physical world, to know how and where we are in time and space. We need to know subconsciously and sometimes consciously if, when, and how energy is moving through the body. While the sensory nervous system lets us know if our eyeball is in our ear or an ant bit our toe, it also often jumps to conclusions based upon what past sensations it has experienced. The perceptive sense of the conscious and subconscious often quite prematurely and amaturely decide for us what is possible in the sea of possibility. We may be in the soulful intention of expansion, but the pre-programmed perceptions in our nervous system may disallow expansive intention from traveling through us.

We experience life because we breathe. Every perception of every moment of our life experience carries with it an associated breathing pattern, and the nervous system is programmed with and by the breath. Every breath we breathe is causal of a perceptive blueprint. As we experience life, these archived patterns of breathing and associated perceptions embedded deep in the nervous system are often triggered by a "like past life experience", or "like soulful intention". Our subconscious breath and nervous system then decide "how it is" before the perceptive sense can freely engage in choice. This often disables us from expanding our perceptive possibilities, as our subconscious neurological system has already decided how we need to feel and *be*. If we repeat these perceptive patterns over time, they become deeply ingrained in our *being*, and limit access to expansive possibility.

The perceptive sense is causal of cognitive thought and action. How our sensory nervous system and perceptive sense are *being* causes our thoughts. The cognitive mind doesn't *really* make our decisions; it just thinks that it does. We can be in the soulful expansion and "cognitive mindset" that anything is possible, but unless the subconscious perception in the sensory nervous system is truly in belief and agreement, our perception will sabotage expansive possibility, and create limiting thoughts and actions. If our *being* feels impossibility in the breath and neurological system, our grandest expansive thoughts are futile. Our physical *being* will disable the cognitive mind.

Contrarily, the breath and nervous system can breathe expansive possibilities through the neurological pathways and change our cognitive thoughts, even if the cognitive mind has decided that expansion is limited or futile. As we breathe space into the subconscious nervous system, we expand the cognitive mind. We are always one great inhalation away from gathering the treasure of possibility from the ashes of limitation.

Although perception is causal of cognition, the cognitive mind and its reason can influence how we feel, breathe, and perceive. The collapse of subconscious/sometimes conscious perception into the cognitive idea of "what is or what is or is not possible" often limits expansion in the transformative process. If the conscious cognitive mind tells us we exist in a small box of limited possibility, we do. The constant cognitive awareness that we exist in restricted space and possibility makes it difficult for us to feel expansion in our soulful breath, nervous system, and causal subconscious perception. We become distant and removed from our expansive power and soulful sense. Our small perceptions then cause small thoughts. This vicious cycle of "small box thinking" becomes the transformative reality of our lives. Ultimately, we can only access the possibilities from the reality that we are *being*. If we "think" and perceive we are limited, we are *being* in limitation.

If both the cognitive and subconscious perceptive sense tell us the world is expansive and infinite, and that the momentary perception we are holding is a mere expandable speck in the sea of possibilities; we feel, breathe, and exist in expansive and powerful.

The universal reality is that perception itself is actually in a constant state of expansion. In that less than a split second, our perceptions and thoughts, both conscious and subconscious, are constantly expanding and collapsing into themselves. If we can identify the things that block and "hold" our perceptions, we can perceive and experience our perceptions as a continually expanding possibility. We can *be* in our soul, breath, body, nervous system, and mind in a way that allows our perceptions to constantly lead to the opening of the soul. We can shift perceptively and neurologically from "what is" to "what is happening, happening, happening".

We simply must train the breath and nervous system to release from holding onto the idea of "what is" in the physical body and world, and allow the *being* and mind to understand that reality is truly expandable. The soulful sense of expansion must constantly feel through the body the mind. As we train ourselves to breathe, feel and think in simultaneity, we are able to perceive the realities of the physical body and world, as we co-exist with the soul in a constant state of expansion. We become the expansion we crave.

*So take a moment or a year and notice how you perceive, not what you perceive. Notice how you perceive expansion?*

Do you perceive your physical body as an expansive changeable entity, or do you "just know" that your body is the way that it is (for example "my hamstrings are tight" or "I just always carry that extra ten pounds" or "my back just hurts".)?

Do you say to yourself, "this is how I am", or ""this is what I do"?

Do you feel that something is possible and then immediately tell yourself all the reasons why it isn't?

Do you tell yourself that anything is possible, but feel that it isn't?

Do you hold tension in your physical body when confronted with change, or do you take a deep breath and smile at the possibility?

Do you hold your breath when you are perceiving or formulating an idea?

Do you perceive expansive possibility as something daunting and unattainable?

Do you perceive that all the possibilities in the world are out there for others, but not for you?

Do you limit possibilities for others, and expect them to act or be a certain way?

Do you "form" your perceptions to justify what you already know?

Do you have ego attached to your opinions, knowledge, and ideas, and fight yourself and others to defend them?

Does your mind tell you that anything is possible?

# Transformation

The transformative space of expansion is a beautiful place to *be*, a place of endless instantaneous choice and possibility. As humans *being*, we know and feel when we are working and *being* with the expansive flow of the universe. Life unfolds like a red carpet, and we choose to walk the path, or simply ask for a green one.

We also know and feel when we are fighting and working against our expansive nature. We find ourselves fighting to unroll life's tapestry only to find it is an undesired design and color.

The way we are *being* expansive in transformation, and our ability to instantaneously choose and manifest our soulfully desired intention is ultimately dependant upon how we move our soulful feeling of expansion from the inside out. This less than a second causal "end" state of transformative expansion is formed by our ability to draw from the sea of possibilities and transfer universal expansion through the soulful sense, the breath, the nervous system, physical body, the perceptive sense and out into the world. As humans *being* we can only transform from where and what we are. Our access to transformative expansion is only as large as our human is *being*.

# **6**

# **Intention**

*" 'Whatever in the world made you think little ant, that you could climb to the top of the Eleph-ant?' snorted Mama Ant.*
*'I didn't think' , said Baby Ant."*

Just imagine for a moment, that you are swimming in the endless sea of possibilities. As you are diving and splashing through countless tiny specks of potential manifestations, your soul's skin is caressed and tickled by what could happen, what should or shouldn't happen, and what needs to be happening in this moment or forever.

Opportunity washes over and through you, at times nearly drowning you in ambiguity. Still, you press on through the waters of overwhelming sensation and confusion in passionate search of the perfect soulful intention, the ultimate shiny sparkle. You feel *it*. You know *it* is there somewhere.

Finally, with a deep breath, you expand into the sea until you find the perfect gem. It's the one! You soulfully know *it*! With all your might, you pull it towards you. . You see it and know it now, the speck that sparkles stronger than all the rest. As you reach to grab it, it pulls away ever so slightly. Again and again, you reach to grasp it, to hold it. Again and again, *it* eludes you.

The next less than a second, you allow yourself to *be* still. You breathe it in. *It* swims towards you, through you.

As it moves closer and closer to your soul, you notice that you dragged with your prize countless other specks of possibility, maybe a bit dimmer in brilliance, but distracting all the same. In simultaneity, you feel the nagging shimmer scratch at your *being* as you willfully pull the pure brightness of your intention of choice deeper towards your soul.

You focus. You feel. You know. And suddenly, in an instant or a year, nothing else matters but the feeling of that single sparkle. Exhaling away the glitter of undesired possibility, you release and fall into the clarity of your diamond. You are left swimming in your precious gem.

This is the nature of intention. As humans *being*, we cannot hold *it*. We may only release into it.

# Stina

Stina somehow knew at the core of her being that she was a singer. As far back as she could remember her head was constantly filled with melodies and words, sometimes so much so and with such intensity that her mind wondered if there was something a bit "crazy" about her. Stina sang constantly in her mind, yet she never heard her own voice. In fact, most of the time, no one ever did.

As a human *being*, Stina was somewhat shy and soft spoken . . . unless; of course, she had something to drink. Then she became so loud that no one could hear her. And she did drink quite a lot now and again, mostly to release her mind from the songs that cried out in her head and the breathless anxiety that lived in her bones. When she was loud she didn't need to sing. When she was loud she couldn't hear herself anyway.

Most certainly, nobody ever knew that Stina sang or could sing; herself included. For years her life had been centered on more practical intentions, "real world" goals of career and family. The possibilities of actually singing seemed remote and distant. She didn't choose to acknowledge them. Yet somehow, she knew deep down inside that she was a singer. The "crazy" songs in her head were a constant reminder.

One moment or year, Stina finally listened. She found herself enrolled in a voice class at college. When asked at the beginning of class why she was there she replied anxiously, "I'm not really sure, I just feel I need to be here. I guess I'd like to sing."

And so it was that the real "craziness" began. As much as Stina soulfully desired to sing, her human *being* would not allow it. At the mere request to make one sound, one harmless passing note in space and time, Stina was overcome with anxiety. She already knew that as soon as she opened her mouth, it would sound loud, terrible, and ugly. As she tried desperately to" hold" her focus and "make the sound happen", her physical body disallowed it. She became short of breath and cried silently in helpless frustration. Instead of releasing soulful vibration through her *being*, she squeaked out a fearful shadow of her heartfelt intention. Although she had never heard it, she hated her own voice. She couldn't even sing to herself when she was alone. She held her breath and thought about singing instead. She cried. While she held the intention to sing, she released her *being* into the intention of fear and holding. Stina truly soulfully desired to release into the power of her voice, yet it was not the true intention of her *being*. The intention of her *being* was to *be* and sound small, and as hard as it was to be this way, it was neurologically and energetically familiar. It was easier to be silent.

Still, Stina soulfully knew she was a singer. She simply did not know how to *be* in singing. Despite many months spent chasing the fear- ridden shadow of her own voice, Stina followed her soul. She diligently began to expand her breath and *being* into the possibility that she could sing, and in time, she slowly released her breath, nervous system, and mind from the parasitic demons that suffocated her soulful intention. She released into and allowed herself to *be* the powerful soulful intention that she is.

A year or so later, Stina is enrolled in music school. Her ability to trust in her subconscious feeling and knowing, and her eventual release into a single soul felt intention has transformed her reality. She is now *being* an amazing and prolific singer songwriter. She sings in the studio, she sings at coffee houses, and sometimes, she even sings to herself. She now inspires singers and humans *being* with the "craziness" in her head and smiles about it.

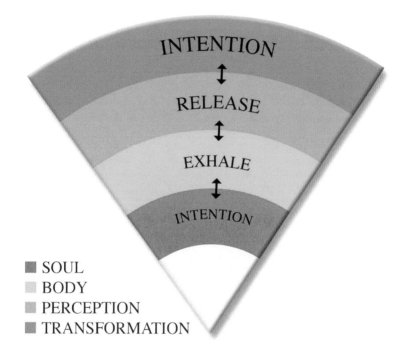

INTENTION
⇕
RELEASE
⇕
EXHALE
⇕
INTENTION

- SOUL
- BODY
- PERCEPTION
- TRANSFORMATION

# The Soul

Intention is not cognitive thought; it is felt. It is soulfully known. Intention, in the soulful sense, is the quantum collapse, the release of our soulful expansion of the infinite into a single possibility of choice. Whether we are aware or unaware, in every less than a second our soul felt intentions choose our reality.

As humans *being*, we crave the power of choice; we crave to soulfully feel our desired reality and subconsciously know that it is possible to manifest it. Innately, we need to follow our soul and choose our true intentions.

Our ability to recognize and release into soulfully desired possibility determines how we *be* in and manifest intention in the physical body and world. Our ability to choose and *be* in intention dictates the transformative choice we experience.

Consciously or subconsciously, soulful intention chooses reality. If we listen to our expansive souls, and allow ourselves to feel, subconsciously know, trust, choose, release into and *be* intention; the power of our intention is now pure transformative choice. We simply need to manifest it.

If we fall out of touch with the soul, our ability to trust our feelings and subconscious knowing is compromised by our life experience, breath, nervous system, and perceptions. This causes our intentions to become cloudy, weak, disempowering, and scattered. Soulful choice becomes random and compromised. We then release into and manifest intentions that are "random and compromised".

Manifestation of "random and compromised" intention renders our *being* paralyzed in soulful confusion. As we fail to expand in possibility and release into soulful intention from the center out, we create holding patterns in the physical body, breath and nervous system. As we hold in fear and ambiguity and the nervous system becomes blocked, it becomes difficult for us to feel who we are and what we truly desire. Confused and unable to access our soulful center, we fight for soulful identity as we search outside of ourselves for our intention and purpose.

Desperate to fill our internal void, we hold intention from the outside in, and can no longer expand and release into internal soulful choice. Subconsciously and sometimes consciously, we then intentionally transform and *be* in causal intentions born of holding, confusion and fear. We breathe, move, live and transform from a basis of fear, holding, and superficiality. This inability to access, trust and release into what we soulfully feel and know greatly limits transformative choice.

As we hold in fear and try to "make" our externally contrived intention a strong and powerful choice, we work against the flow of the ever-expanding universe. We hold the cognitive idea of our soulful intention in our head, but we are unable to truly feel it or release it through our soul and body from the inside out. We may cognitively perceive we are in soulfully chosen intention, when in actuality we are miles away from accessing it or moving it through our *being*.

Not only must we release into our desired soulful intention; we must release from all intention that interferes with it. Even if we feel and know what our chosen intention is, as we breathe to release into it, we may find that with it comes some "unintentional baggage". The parasitic possibilities of weak desire, right or wrong decision, and scattered choice often become embedded in our nervous system and psyche. They cling desperately to transformative choice, eating away the clarity of intention, and the power to release into soul-felt decision.

Thankfully, we exist as humans *being*, and our breath is a constant link and access to expansive possibility and soulful choice. As ruler of the nervous system, our breath has the power to release any barriers that inhibit the process of *being* in and choosing soulful intention. We simply must, moment by moment, believe and soulfully know that because we breathe, we can, in any instant, access and release into the power of our soulful intention. As we learn *be* in our breath in a way that allows us to *feel* the expanse of universal power and choice, our chosen soulful intention is only one breath away from transformative reality.

*So take a moment or a year to be in your soulful intentions.*

Do you really soulfully know and feel your intentions?

Do you trust your own soul?

Do you feel your intentions matter?

Are your thoughts and intentions incongruent?

Are you carrying the heavy weight of emotional baggage?

Are there unwanted possibilities attached to your intentions?

Are you unable to release into what you really want?

Do you feel fear, anxiety, or anger at the mere idea of delving into your feelings?

Can you feel release?

Do you soulfully know that you are the power of choice?

# The Body

Although soulful intention and transformative choice begin at the root of the soul, we are humans *being* in the physical world. This situation of the human meat-suit condition dictates that our soulful intentions must pass through the framework of the human body and nervous system to exist as our reality. If the pathway of the human body is open and the breath and nervous system release into the soulful intention of choice, this true soulful intention becomes transformative choice in the physical body and world.

Intention in the physical body correlates to the exhale. Exhalation releases both the autonomic and somatic nervous systems. Not only do we rid ourselves of $CO_2$ and other toxins as we exhale, we release holding and over stimulation in our neurological patterning, leaving a clear pathway for desired change. Because the breath controls the nervous system, which controls everything we think, do or experience; a released exhalation and nervous system means we have real and tangible access to transformative soulful choice, both in the physical body and life.

Unfortunately and fortunately, the most common physical block in the transformative process occurs in exhalation. As humans *being* in the "real world", we are breathing through every moment. Our life experiences, such as pain, euphoria, trauma, frustration, concentration, and emotional stresses are subconsciously/sometimes consciously connected with our breathing patterns, and thus connected to our neurological abilities to release into and facilitate desired transformative intention and change. Holding patterns in exhalation, whatever the type or cause, not only clog the nervous system with undesired tension and intention; these holding patterns limit the expansive possibilities of the following inhalation. As we continue to hold in a bit on every subsequent exhale, our physical transformative channels become more and more clogged. We feel less space, less opportunity, less power of choice. We physically hold against our power to choose. Soulful intention has difficulty breaking through these physical barriers, and our intentional reality is compromised.

Just as fear holds in the soul and body preventing expansion; traumatic life experiences hold in the soul and body, preventing release. Perceived pain, stress, fear, or lack of control in the physical body and world cause the breath and nervous system pull in with fear and protect.

As humans *being*, our bodies are equipped with a defense mechanism called "fight or flight". Our subconscious in the hindbrain (medulla oblongata) engages this mechanism when the nervous system perceives stress. When we feel fear, the hindbrain releases stress hormones that send out a message of distress to the body and tell it to speed up the heart rate and speed up the breath. This message literally tells the lungs to speed up inhalation and suck in as much oxygen in as possible. As inhalation speeds up, exhalation becomes harder to release. When exhalation does not fully release, the subsequent inhale becomes more difficult to expand…. a vicious cycle. We become neurologically stuck on the inhalation, grasping for breath, holding in. Release becomes secondary, sometimes almost non-existent.

While this awesome lifesaving "fight or flight" feature is greatly advantageous in the event of a bear attack, this mechanism leaves in its wake patterns of neurological holding in exhalation. These subconscious holding patterns of panic can then be triggered by the mildest experience…the dropping of a coffee cup or the sharp words of a loved one. In severe cases, these holding patterns manifest as panic attacks, anxiety disorder, or post- traumatic stress syndrome. For most of us, this simply means that subconsciously we hold or speed up our inhalations and fail to fully release our exhalations when we are consciously or subconsciously confronted with any type of perceptively "stressful situation". Even if we feel, know, and choose the greatest of soulful intentions, the holding in the breath and nervous system may not allow us to release into them and gain access to transformative choice. This leaves us literally physically unable to get *in* our intention.

The good news is that because we experience "fight or flight", we are wired to access and change the patterning of the subconscious nervous system through our breath. Our breath is the only life sustaining mechanism in the physical body that is both conscious and subconscious, voluntary and involuntary. With practice, we can consciously control our breath and change our subconscious breathing patterns. Because of this conscious subconscious link, we can access, clear, and re-program the subconscious nervous system through the conscious intentions of our inhalation and exhalation.  Through focused release in exhalation, we can clear the nervous system, release from neurological barriers and holding patterns, and clear the way for efficient neurological pathways, productive kinesthetic patterning, and soulful transformative choice to move freely through us. We literally possess the ability to exhale and rewire our physical *being* to accept and release into our transformative intention of choice.

The reality of this is amazing! As humans *being* in the gift of the breath and soulful intention, we have within us the power to transform our physical structure, our movement patterning, our thoughts, our moods, our behaviors, our lives, and our world!

*So take a moment or a year to notice how you are being in exhalation.*

Do you fully release in exhalation?

Do you force or blow air out, or does it calmly and gracefully leave your lungs?

Does tension in your throat or chest make it difficult to release?

Do you forget to exhale when you are concentrating, frustrated, stressed, or angry?

Do you experience tension in exhalation when you are in physical exertion?

Do you have chronic pain, TMJ, fibromyalgia, muscle spasms, back pain, Parkinson's disease, anxiety, depression, cancer, asthma, digestive issues, or high blood pressure?

Does it seem next to impossible to increase your flexibility?

Are you resistant to change?

# Perception

The perceptive sense in intention is a foggy mirror that reflects truths and untruths. Whatever the subconscious nervous system tells the mind to think, based on how the intention of choice did or did not move through the soul, breath and nervous system; the perceptive mind, consciously and subconsciously believes to be true.The mind then takes this as truth; and in a split second tells us that this is reality, the "result" of our soulful intention.

This reflection of the perception back to the nervous system can work for us or against us. While it is necessary for the mind to let us subconsciously and cognitively know how intention is translating through and into the physical body and world; that same knowledge can keep the nervous system in a continual state of holding, and prevent the mind from allowing soulful choice as a possibility.

Just imagine for a moment that you soulfully desire to release and stretch your hamstrings and touch your toes. You take a great big inhale, exhale, and bend forward. You feel the sensation and then your mind says "Oh! My hamstrings are tight!"

In that split second, your mind just told your nervous system that your hamstrings are, in fact, actually tight. You are now *being*, in that instant, in tight hamstrings. This *being* causes your neurological system to fire and *be* in tightness and resistance. The soulful intention of choice, released hamstrings becomes compromised. You are now subconsciously and consciously perceiving yourself as a human *being* with tight hamstrings, and as your cognitive mind knows, "Tight hamstringed humans can't touch their toes!"

This perception in your cognitive mind and nervous system not only squashes your chosen intention; it diminishes your soulful access to all possibilities of flexibility and release. Your muscle fibers hold, *being* in tension. This becomes yet another vicious neurological cycle. Your mind tells your breath, body and soul that you *are* "tight", and thus desired transformative intention of choice, release, becomes impossibility.

But is it really impossible? Imagine, that in another moment, you soulfully intend to release your hamstrings. You inhale, exhale, and release your body to forward bend. You notice the sensation of tightness in your hamstrings and hips, but you simultaneously instantaneously breathe and expand into the intention and sensation of release. You soulfully know that you will feel and are feeling release. This breath now tells the nervous system that the intention of choice, "release", may override the perceptive sense of the mind, "tightness". The "tightness" of your hamstrings no longer matters. You expanded through your perception. You are now *being* the intention of release through your entire body, hamstrings included, and well on the path to touching your toes!

Thankfully, we know that ultimately soulful intention is what drives true transformative choice and change; not perception or the mind. The truth is somewhere in the mirror, we must simply *feel* through the fog of conscious and cognitive perception, and subconsciously *feel and know* our intention is true. We must experience subconscious and sometimes conscious perception, but breathe and *be* in soulful intention. If we can release from holding perception, and feel and *be* in our intention of choice as we "experience" cognitive perception, we can begin to breathe, release, and be in our nervous systems in a manner that clears the fog. Focused intention is then crystal clear. We gain clear access to the breath, neurological systems and transformative choice. We now choose what and how we perceive.

*So take a moment or a year to notice how you perceive in intention.*

Do your perceptions support your soulful intentions or block them?

Does your mind constantly kick in and pull you from sensation?

Do your perceptions continually resist change?

Does your mind fixate?

Do you perceive that you are doing one thing, and find yourself doing another?

Are you a "logical" thinker?

Do you perceive that you *should* be doing one thing, but do another?

Does the mere act of perception or cognitive thought cause tension in your physical body, or holding in your breath?

Do you truly perceive and know the power and choice of your intentions?

Do you perceive that in every breath you have soulful choice?

Are you afraid of the power of soulful choice?

# Transformation

As humans being, we are choosing our intentions with every breath. With every less than a split second of our existence, we are always intending something, aware or unaware. How our intentions exist in and manifest our reality is a result of how we choose them and transfer them through our human being.

Transformative intention exists in a constant instantaneous state of release; the release into our power that allows us, in awareness, to soulfully choose intention from the expansive sea of possibilities. In transformative intention, we let go of any other possibilities, perceptions, or neurological baggage that interfere with the intention of choice. This requires us to release all barriers in the soul, breath, nervous system and mind, and allow this soulful sense of *being* to shine through our human. In the transformative sense, we do not make, have, or hold intentions. We *are* them.

When we are truly *being* soulful transformative intention, intention itself becomes malleable, expandable. It expands and collapses our entire human form and energy. As we flow through the sea of possibilities, our *being* expands in grace as we release from one intention to the next. Our chosen path is undeniably clear.

**7**

# Manifestation

*"Eleph-ant asked Baby Ant who tickled the top of his head....
'How could you possibly climb all the way up here?'
"How could I possibly not?" replied Baby Ant."*

Just imagine for a moment that you are sitting on your back deck, feeling soulfully desired intention moving through you. You chose and released into that bright purple sparkly gem, the one that flows through you and inspires you to plant those beautiful spring petunias in your back yard. You take in a deep breath, close your eyes, and exhale. Everything is purple. You bathe in the softness of iridescent violet petals as you feel your hands gently plant them lovingly in the moist ground. You can smell them.

In the next moment, day, or year, your neighbor pops by and gives you his extra flat of purple petunia plants. He just saw them and thought of you. Soulfully inspired, you thank him, and immediately without a second thought you rush to the neighborhood nursery to purchase another flat of the beauties.

Before you know it, there you are in the backyard, elbow deep in moist soil and flowery purple flesh. You feel, you plant; and when the last seed of soulful intention is safely rooted, you take a rest by the garden and take it all in.

Wide eyed, you inhale, exhale, and *be*. Everything is purple. You bathe in the softness of iridescent violet, as you gently caress the petals of manifestation. You smile. You knew you would *be* here.

# Mark

Mark could manifest anything. An all around nice guy, self -made businessman, stellar athlete and entrepreneur; he was the epitome of boundless energy, self- discipline, and tenacious will. By the age of forty-five he had manifested a comfortable house in the mountains, numerous entrepreneurial business, a beautiful family, and comfortable lifestyle.

Mark worked hard and played hard. He was an expert skier, an avid mountain biker, and spent most of his free time enjoying and conquering the great outdoors. His competitive edge and fiery determination led him to find success in just about everything he touched. Mark did not believe in failure, even in fun; in fact, self admittedly, he didn't really believe in much unless it was backed up with tangible factual knowledge. He was not entirely skeptical; yet his extremely analytical mind simply didn't allow much space for any esoteric fluff. In his mind, life was what he made it. If he did believe in anything, he believed that with hard work and discipline he could make anything happen...and he did.

As he rounded the corner of age fifty, Mark began to manifest something new; debilitating back pain. Not that he had not experienced a bit of back pain off and on over the years as the result of overuse, stress, or the occasional wipeout on his skis or bike. He did have the occasional flare up due to the intensity or stress of his life; but up until this point, had always managed to push through and conquer the pain of it. This new pain was something new and different. It was completely excruciating and seemingly unconquerable. It hurt to get out of bed in the morning, it hurt to sit and work, and it became so uncomfortable to ski or engage in intense physical activity that Mark began to forego all of the sports he so deeply loved. In time, he became physically weak, depressed and frustrated. Lack of physical movement and disengagement from the activities that fed his soul left him devastated.

Mark was, however, the kind of person who could make anything happen. Helpless he was not. If there were a problem, he would find the solution, and like any great successful intellectual mind, Mark sought help. He engaged in western medical intelligence and began to understand the degenerative nature of his inter

-vertebral discs. He received massages and manual bodywork. He went to physical therapy and learned about his causal postural imbalances. He constantly analyzed his alignment and muscle imbalance, sometimes quite literally to the point of pain, and religiously practiced the assigned corrective exercises. Mark knew one thing. If he tried hard enough, he would make himself better. He would make the pain go away.

Yet, as hard as he tried to cognitively understand his back problem, and with discipline correct his physical imperfections, Mark could not find any real relief. Despite the factual knowledge that there was nothing seriously wrong with his spine, and the great disciplined effort he focused in his structural rehabilitation, nothing he did could make his pain go away. If anything, the harder he tried, the more it hurt. The more it hurt, the more he focused on the pain. Eventually, he became the manifestation of his engagement with pain. Mark was miserable.

As somewhat of a last resort to retrieve his youth and active lifestyle, Mark sought me out as a yoga therapist. His first words to me were:

" Just to let you know.... I don't really know anything about this yoga stuff! I am willing to try it, but I truly don't believe in any of it. At this point, however, I will try and do anything. I just want to make it better. I want my life back!"

I knew at this point that this was definitely my cue to take the scientific analytical route. We began with a discussion of quantum physics and causal energy, and moved on to breath and energy transfer and the causal energies of the subconscious and conscious nervous system. We chatted about anatomical alignment, subconscious skeletal stabilization, and holding patterns in the breath and neurological systems. We talked about how energy engages in the nervous system and moves through kinesthetic chain. We even touched upon the phenomenon of the psycho-energetic systems as they relate to the physical energetic systems of the body.

When Mark's cognitive mind was somewhat satisfied with ideas and logic, we began the process of analysis of his breath and movement patterning. Through this process we discovered that Mark manifested more than he thought he did. Much more. Alongside his many obvious accomplishments and abilities to focus and create desired change in his life, Mark had subconsciously manifested some deep- rooted blocks and holding patterns in his breath, neurological, and skeletal systems. Although his go- getter nature led to successful manifestation in many realms, and he was quite engaged, if not over-engaged in the act of manifestation; the manner in which he engaged in manifestation was quite aggressive and lacked grounded center. Instead of releasing into his intention, engaging in it from the center of his being, and allowing it to flow freely through him, Mark constantly held intention and forced manifestation to happen through his breath and body with the sheer power of his iron will. Mark engaged in his body and life in subconscious holding and force. He was so good at it that even managed to smile as he did it.

After many years of held breath, forced physical exertion through improper skeletal alignment, kinesthetic misfire, and overuse of superficial musculature, Mark could no longer release his nervous system or engage in the subconscious stabilization of his skeletal structure enough to ease his pain. Like many humans who experience long term inexplicable back pain and spasm, Mark's nervous system subconsciously fired in pain and holding for no reason at all. The constant subconscious/sometimes conscious expectation that there could or would be pain manifested fear and holding in his breath and nervous system. This holding caused muscle spasm and thus, "real" pain. The experience of pain, and the fear of it caused further holding in the breath and nervous system, thus manifesting more of the same; pain. The more focused effort he exerted to "fix" himself, the more effort itself caused the pain.

Like many real solutions, the answers lie in the questions themselves. As much as it was Mark's habit and subconscious nature to "make" himself better, the solution to his back pain lay in the release of his present breathing and movement patterning and the reprogramming of his subconscious nervous system. He did not need to alter the pain he manifested; he needed to simply change how he was engaging in and being in manifestation itself. He needed to do less, release more, and allow his breath, nervous system, and musculature to subconsciously engage from the core of his being.

From that day on, Mark focused the gift of his intensity and will into release and the engagement of center. Somewhere around the time of his fifth session he felt the power of his centered being move from his pelvis through his nervous and skeletal systems and release him from his pain. Excitedly, he smiled and laughed and said,

"I still don't really know how this yoga thing works, but it does! Its really weird, but it does! All I do is breathe and focus on that feeling, and it works! No pain... strange! I didn't really do anything except breathe, release, and engage!"

Remarkably, Mark didn't feel in that moment as though he needed to formulate any logical answer to his newly discovered solution. All he wanted to do was take his newfound way of being and manifest it on the ski hill... and so, he did!

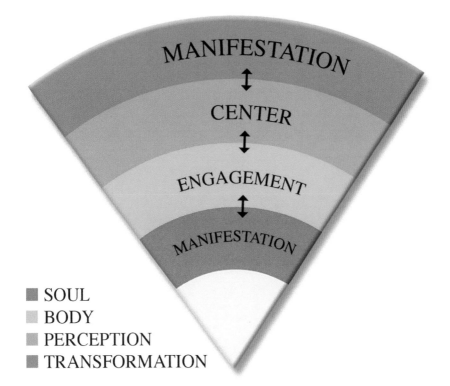

SOUL
BODY
PERCEPTION
TRANSFORMATION

# The Soul

As part of the expanding transformative universe, the soul itself is in a constant state of manifestation. Our soulful sense and subconscious feeling and knowing literally manifest themselves. As the universe is expanding and releasing into "happening", we too, with our soulful intentions expand and release to create our physical bodies and world. This manifestation is inevitable. As humans being, aware or unaware we are constantly manifesting. How the soul is *being* in manifestation determines our ability to manifest chosen intention in the physical body and world.

Manifestation in the soulful sense is the deep subconscious knowing and feeling that we have the ability to create; to take the power of our chosen intention and literally "engage in and allow" it to happen in the physical body and physical world.

Soulful manifestation is a choice. The greatest of soulful intentions are just that, great soulful intentions until they are manifested through us and create our reality. If intention is clear and we soulfully feel, trust, release and engage in our power to manifest, we can create and transform anything.

The soulful ability to feel centered and take action from a fixed point of intention allows us to decide what and how it is we are manifesting. As humans *being* in manifestation, we can only come from and be from where we are. We must soulfully know where and why we are coming and *being* from. As we choose our intention from the sea of universal possibilities, we must instantaneously release into it and engage in the possibility of manifesting it. This engagement allows intention to become chosen reality. Spiritually and emotionally, we need to feel and engage in the universal center from which all manifestation is happening.

The soulful path to manifestation must be clear. Conscious or subconscious feelings of fear, doubt, anger, or helplessness often over-ride soulful intention and the power to engage in manifestation. These negative holding patterns in the soulful emotive sense cause blockage and holding patterns in our breath, physical body and nervous system. These physical blocks, in turn, compromise our ability to truly feel, access, and allow soulful intention to engage in our being.

In a state of physical or emotional compromise, we attempt to force intention through and "make things happen". This forcing of manifestation causes us to work against the expansive nature and flow of universal causal energy. As we hold in and force our *being* we stifle organic expansion from the inside out. This limits our capacity to access, engage in, and manifest transformative power and desired change. Contrary to our western belief system, we do not "make" soulful intentions happen. We release into them, engage in them, and allow them to become.

However we are engaged in manifestation and whatever we choose, we manifest.

If we are soulfully engaging from center in love, truth, prosperity and soulfully chosen intention; we manifest love, truth, prosperity, and soulfully chosen intention.

If we are soulfully engaging in fear, doubt, anger, or helplessness; we manifest fear, doubt, anger, and helplessness, regardless of the soulful intention we think we are manifesting.

Ultimately, the soul and breath are the causal forces in the human condition. If we soulfully choose and intend to *be* in empowered manifestation, we will be. This soulful knowing that we have the ability to breathe into, engage in, and manifest anything will instantaneously or eventually break down any perceived barriers or limitations: emotional, physical or neurological.

We feel, we breathe. We allow, we engage, we manifest, we become.

> *So take a moment or a year and soulfully feel your power to manifest.*

Do you feel you can manifest anything you choose?

Do you feel the power to create change in you physical body and life?

Do you think and fantasize about goals, but never achieve them?

Do you experience "fear of success"?

Do you often feel unmotivated or paralyzed?

Are you motivated by fear or anger?

Are you envious and jealous of others?

Do you feel creative?

Are you engaged in and excited about your everyday life?

Do you expect others to change your world for you?

Do you love the things you do and create?

Are you easily distracted from your intentions?

Do you feel that things are easier for others?

Are you an under-achiever?

Are you an over-achiever?

# The Body

As a reality of humans *being*, we get to engage in the human body and manifest through it. Manifestation requires physical engagement of the human *being*. Every soulful intention, conscious or subconscious, must pass through the human systems on its path to perceived reality.

Manifestation in the physical body and physical world occurs in that less than a split second when soulful intention releases through the breath and engages the nervous system. Literally, how we consciously and subconsciously engage intention through the breath and physical body determines what and how we manifest in the physical world.

As a part of the expanding universe, our physical *beings* are, like everything else, in a constant state of expansion and collapse. There exists in the body an energetic center point from which we expand, freely release, and manifest our physical *being* out into the world.

If we are engaged, rooted, and balanced in this physical center, we collapse easily into our chosen reality and manifest freely through ourselves in alignment with universal expansion.

If we do not engage and balance our physical body from this center energy we become misaligned, and cannot expand and release freely through ourselves. Manifestation becomes forced and contorted.

In the physical body, engagement in manifestation begins at the root of the pelvis, both anatomically and psycho-energetically. The root of the pelvis is the fulcrum, the center point from which intention moves. However we release intention from the breath and engage intention from this center point determines our physical, emotional and cognitive power to create.

In the skeletal muscular system, how we engage or disengage in the pelvis determines our stabilization of center, structural alignment and neurological movement patterning. All of the bones, muscles, connective tissues and fascia of the body directly or indirectly attach at some point to the pelvis. How we engage anatomically through the fulcrum of the pelvis determines what happens in our shoulders, fingers, knees, toes…. even our organs and ears. All of this affects our posturing, our muscular holding patterns and our nervous system.

Stabilization of the entire skeletal system is both a conscious and sub-conscious neurological process. This means that we are always sub-consciously firing in our neurological system to stand, stabilize, engage and move, but we also have conscious choice of how we stand, stabilize, engage and move. Through conscious choice, we can, through the neurological pathway of the breath, teach the subconscious nervous system to stabilize and manifest from center engagement.

The deep muscles of the pelvis and neurological awareness in the pelvic floor dictate how we find and be in center in the physical body. If we can find center engagement in the pelvis, both consciously and subconsciously, the neurological system feels engaged, focused, safe, and ready for action and change. Our external musculature flows freely around a centered axis.

If the physical body is not engaged and expanding from the pelvic center out, we fall out of center alignment both consciously and sub-consciously, and our external structure holds in fear to support us. The superficial musculature of the body becomes over engaged, and the deep muscles that are meant to engage in stabilization atrophy. This causes the breath and nervous system to hold. The more we hold in to support ourselves, the less we are able to feel and find center engagement; which causes further holding.

This holding and *being* in the body from the outside in makes it difficult for us to engage intention through the body from the inside out in a centered, rooted source of manifestive power. As we physically engage in a structure of confusion, tension, misalignment and instability, we subconsciously/sometimes consciously feel confusion, tension and instability. Our physical body tells us that we are not fully engaged and ready to manifest. We hold. We force. Our physical bodies literally work against engaging in and releasing into manifestation of soulful intention.

In the emotional subtle energies of the psycho-energetic system, chakra system, manifestation also begins at the root of the pelvis or "muladhara chakra". In this root chakra lives our raw human power, our right to be *being* in this world. In the root chakra we exist in either confidence or fear. When fully engaged from the psycho energetic root of our *being*, we manifest and move intention through ourselves with the utmost confidence. When disengaged in the muladhara, everything we manifest is born from a basis of fear. However we engage, mis-engage, or disengage in the muladhara forms our basis of emotional and psychological manifestation. As the root of our psycho-energetic system, engagement in this center is necessary for the soulful manifestation of anything: emotion, power, love, creativity, and spiritual growth.

Our psycho-energetic systems are causal in our physical *being*. If we are engaging in fear, apathy, or disengagement in our root chakra, our physical body and *being* also engages in and from fear, apathy, and disengagement. The breath is compromised, and centered manifestive power is diminished. As we physically engage in this fear and inaction, the body and nervous system subconsciously create holding patterns or blocks centered in these feelings. Often times this psycho-energetic pelvic prison literally disallows us from physically manifesting what we soulfully want. Even if the intention in our soul and breath is "purely manifestable", consciously or subconsciously our emotional blocks and lack of engagement in the subconscious nervous system and physical structure may disable it. We try endlessly to break out and "make things happen" but somehow find ourselves physically, emotionally, and mentally unable to engage and soulfully manifest.

Even if we do "force through and achieve" our physical world goals, we often find ourselves feeling half full and dissatisfied. Manifestation from over engagement or mis-engagement leads us further away from the true essence of our intention. Internally empty, we seek to fill and engage our center from the outside in through our ego: the external stimulation of our "achievement" and our cognitive idea of our existence in the superficial material world. Our *being* becomes tight, held, polluted, and often ill, or in dis-ease. We feel physically and mentally trapped as we manifest from the shell of what we are, and create more of what we are; a shell of our desired intention. Access to the soulful sense is diminished, and heartfelt desired action becomes limited and difficult. In this neurologically compromised state of *being*, we create a vicious cycle of compromised engagement, manifestive misery, and undesired choice.

The beautiful thing is that as soulful breathing humans, we have the power to break through any barriers of manifestation we create. Through the breath and release of the nervous system, we can find center. We can consciously teach the subconscious to engage and move our physical *being* from center, both psycho-energetically and anatomically.

We simply need to recognize our own emotional and physical neurological patterns and obstacles, and engage in the soulful desire to free ourselves from them. We must intend and *be* in the feeling and power of physically centered manifestation, and breath by breath, send soulful intention through the nervous system to release us from our physical and neurological prisons. Once we literally free ourselves from ourselves; we can fully physically engage and *be manifesting* in chosen soulful intention and manifestative power. We literally become our soulful intention.

*So take a moment or a year to notice how your body engages in manifestation.*

Is it stressful for you to move your body and just *be* everyday?

Are you lethargic or hyper-active?

Do you have high blood pressure?

Do you become immobilized in times of stress?

Are you tense and tight when you feel you need to "make things happen?

Do you often hold your breath, especially in doing or thinking?

Do you experience back pain, sciatica, heartburn, stomach ulcers, cancer, cramping or insomnia?

Do you have high blood pressure?

Do you feel uncoordinated?

Are you accident -prone?

Do you move in "parts", or does your movement flow gracefully from center?

Do you become ill either during or after a big deadline?

Are you able to manifest change in your own physical body?

Do you feel you want one thing, but your mind and body do something else?

Do you get physically released only to tighten right back up again?

Do you ever feel like you literally can't get past yourself?

# Perception

Perceptive sense in manifestation dictates how we create the fascia of our cognitive reality. Cognitive reality often tells us what is possible or impossible to manifest. Although soulful intention is the causal source of manifestation in the expanding universe, and the physical body is the vehicle, the perceptive sense, both consciously and subconsciously often dictates *if* and *how* soulful intention of choice is manifesting. Perception in our subconscious nervous system drives our thoughts which most often choose our actions. How we are *being* in subconscious/ sometimes conscious perception in manifestation determines *if* and *what* we manifest.

We perceive from what we are and what we manifest. We perceive from who we are *being* and how we are manifesting. As humans *being*, we can only *be* and become from where we are. If we are soulfully and physically engaged in the center of manifestation, we will perceive center, and manifest freely from center. If we are disengaged, mis-engaged, or over engaged in the soul and body, we will perceive lack of center and instability in manifestation, and manifest from fear, apathy, confusion, or stress.

We become and create only what we perceive is possible in manifestation. Just as the soul and physical body are causal of perception, our perceptive *being* is causal of manifestation in the body, soul, and reality. If the subconscious/ sometimes-conscious mind perceives that we are engaged in centered manifestation, and truly knows that we have the ability to manifest desired intention; manifestation in the soul, breath, neurological system, and body is possible. If the subconscious/ sometimes- conscious mind perceives and believes impossibility of manifestation; regardless whether manifestation is truly possible or not, perception will shut down the nervous system, and literally create impossibility for desired transformation or change in the physical body and physical world.

Quite often, our perceptive images are skewed. Spiritual, emotional, and physical holding patterns greatly affect our nervous system, and thus what the minds eye perceives. The subconscious soul, breath, nervous system and body supply the backdrop of our perceptive realities. When the perceptive pathways are clear and the backdrop untainted, we perceive what we truly manifest, and we manifest from clarity. If the subconscious backdrop is clouded with unreleased life experiences, spiritual, physical and emotional graffiti, we experience altered perceptions of what we manifest, and we manifest from altered perception and confused reality.

Every less than a split second, the gift of perception offers us a snapshot of our reality, a glimpse into the process and result of our soulfully chosen manifestation. If our perceptive sense is centered and expansive, these pictures of our created reality flow over and through us as we simultaneously manifest. Quite often, however, due to holding patterns in the nervous system and subconscious perception, the conscious or subconscious mind becomes fixated on a particular image. As we grasp onto this perceptive image, the cognitive mind chimes in to judge what it means. We become stuck in our heads, repeating the same image over and over, endlessly trapped in our own thinking. This holds up the flow of manifestation.

As the perceptive mind consciously or subconsciously fixates, the cognitive mind takes over, and the physical body and soulful sense disconnect from the manifestive process. The feel and flow of intention is lost. We find ourselves "perceiving" or" judging" about what just happened or cognitively "thinking" about what will happen and how we are manifesting and *being*; instead of just "feeling, *being* and doing" what is happening. Our human *being* is no longer engaged in the center of soulful manifestation. The thoughts take over, judgment is passed, and the process of soulful manifestation is blocked.

With this perceptive disconnection from the manifestive process comes further holding in the breath, body, and soul. This causes the entire transformative process to feel strained and difficult. As we feel and perceive strain and difficulty in manifestation, the cognitive mind kicks in and begins to "brainwash" us into believing that it is simply difficult to make anything happen. The brain tells the nervous system, breath, and body that manifestation is just too hard, too impossible, and so; it is.

As humans *being*, when we perceive and *be* in "manifestation is impossible or difficult", we cognitively decide we must either "try harder to make something happen", or give up and "check out". This *being* in perceptive trying or apathy disallows us from releasing physically or spiritually into centered engagement. We manifest from either force or disengagement, neither of which serves our soulful intention.

Thankfully, however, it is possible to recognize and break through the perceptive barriers of manifestation. Every less than a second our breath and body give us clues as to whether or not our perceptions are serving our soulful manifestation. If our perceptions are consciously or subconsciously limiting manifestation, our soul, breath, and body will manifest and feel limitation.

As we open to and *be* in our soul, breath, and body, we feel and release into the power of our manifestive center. From this power of center engagement we create the physical causal energy of our soulful intention, and clear our neurological pathways. This causes our perceptions to become expansive, clear, and fluidSnapshot images of what is and what is possible flow over us as soulful intention manifests through us. As we perceive ourselves manifesting soulful intention, we do just that, and become desired transformation. Our perceptive sense then acts as a guide of manifestation instead of a cognitive dictator of possibility. The mind frees us to *be*.

*So take a moment or a year to notice how you manifest in perception.*

Do you find yourself stuck in your head and trapped by your thoughts?

Do your pre-conceived perceptions, beliefs, and past experiences dictate what and how you choose to manifest?

Do you manifest and then immediately "know" how it is?

Do you know what you manifest?

Are your manifestations in alignment with your perceptions of them?

Do you perceive and immediately seek the cognitive explanation of your perception?

Do you allow yourself to "expand your reality", or do you just "know how it is"?

Are your perceptions often different from what others say is really happening?

Do you soulfully "know" what is manifested, but perceive something else?

Do you manifest from your gut feelings?

Are you satisfied with what you manifest?

*So take a moment or a year to notice how you manifest in perception.*

Is the glass "half full" or "half empty"?

Do you experience headaches, neck and jaw tension, anorexia, bulimia, or T.M.J?

Do you have poor balance?

# Transformation

Manifestation is transformative when soulful intention flows, releases, and engages effortlessly from the center of humans *being*. Transformative manifestation creates the inertia that spins chosen intention through our physical systems and out into the world. However we engage and manifest through our soul, body, perceptions, and *being* determines our transformative power in manifestation. As we soulfully choose and engage in *if, what, why, and how* we manifest, we transform not only our own humans *being*, we manifest the transformative power of our world.

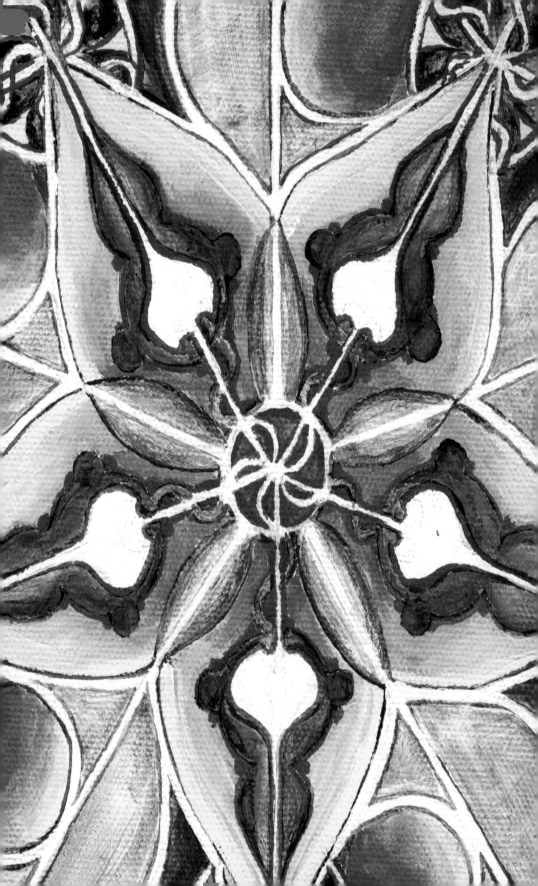

**8**

# Energy

*" 'However did you find the energy to climb all the way up here crazy little ant?' asked the Eleph-ant.*
*'I never lost it,' explained Baby Ant.*
*'Still, you must be weary from your journey.' consoled Eleph-ant.*
*'I can't imagine walking such a distance!'*
*'Oh no!' exclaimed Baby Ant.*
*'Its much more work to stand still like you do!' "*

Just imagine for a moment you are standing on top of a world that is spinning, and in your hand you hold a spinning top. As you stand perceptively still as your world spins, you take the top between your fingers and spin it. It drops to the floor and miraculously it stands up, grounded in flight by the center energy that you created.

Through child's eyes you watch it for a moment, mesmerized by the perceptively invisible force that flies from its surface and suspends it in space. For a split moment, it seems to expand and manifest beyond itself. It bleeds from the center out into the surrounding space until suddenly, without warning, it slows and begins to collapse into itself. It shrinks. It wobbles. In a mere second, it transforms itself from a vibrant *being* into a perceptively dull lifeless little piece of wood.

Lovingly, you pick it up from the floor, and gaze down at its frozen shape in your hand. There it lies, raw energy crying out for center inertia.

It begs you to spin it. You smile, take a breath, and release it out through your fingers, causing the top to once again, happily spin and ground itself to the earth.

Again you watch and notice, drawn inward by the energy that flies out from the center point. For a split second, you breathe with the top, and feel how you stand suspended in space, rooted to the ground, expanding out from your center inertia as the earth spins you.

Such is the nature of energy. It is in, through, and of everything; the cause and result of all manifestation; raw transformation crying to be spun.

# Seth

Seth sat hunched on the leather sofa and covered his ears with his hands. She was screaming at him again, just like the kids at school. Everyone always screamed at him.

"Seth! Get your lazy ass off the couch right now and take out the garbage!" yelled his mother. "Are you listening? Now!"

Seth groaned and squeezed at his ears a little harder. He focused on his video game, and dove deep into his cyber world. No one could touch him here. Here, he was safe. He zoned in, released his hands, and became only vaguely aware of the nagging reality of background noise that echoed down the hall. Here he sat spread out on the couch, all five foot two 289 lbs of him, engrossed, mesmerized by his tiny box world. Here, he was the hero. Here, he could run and jump and climb better than even Jake, the strongest boy at school. No one called him fat and lazy or any of the countless other names *they* used to sap his energy. Here, in the safety of his adipose shell and cyber world, he was invincible. Here he was in control. No one could touch his soul, especially himself. His adrenalin rushed as he conquered in complete stillness, except, of course for the ceaseless tapping of his right foot. His foot always tapped. He took out a few villains, climbed a mountain, and ran all the way to the finish...just in time...he scored! He won! For a moment he breathed and basked in the euphoria of the flashing victory emblem. For a moment, he was powerful.

And then, in less than a second everything went quiet. He took the last gulp of his cola, sank back into his familiar dent in the couch, and closed his eyes. The entire house was eerily silent, aside from the stifled wheeze of his breath as his tiny lungs fought to feed the immense girth of his body. He sighed in troubled annoyance, irritated by the calm, and the subliminal power of his breath. He noticed his foot tapping. For less than a second, he wondered why it kept doing that. He tried to stop it and then gave up. He was powerless in that department. It didn't matter anyway. Even his own mother had given up on him. Again, he sighed.

"Maybe I should just get up off the couch and go take the trash out…or…maybe not," he thought.

He sank deeper into the sofa. He felt tired, lazy, bored. He wished he were different, that his world was different, but it wasn't; and anyway, he certainly didn't have the energy to change it. It wasn't so bad to be a bit heavy. At least he wasn't like those skinny anorexic teenage girls who had to run everyday. Now that would be bad. His foot tapped more aggressively just thinking about it.

Another listless sigh reverberated through his fleshy being as he finally resigned himself to pull his heavy weight up from the couch. He held his breath and grunted as he hoisted the immense mass of his eleven year old *being* to its feet. Funny… he noticed. When he was standing and walking his foot couldn't tap. He forced a miserable smile, and in the best of intentions, he ambled heavily towards the kitchen for the trashcan. Somehow, he found himself in front of the refrigerator. Instantaneously, Seth began to cry.

And from that moment on, Seth cried a lot. The harder he cried, the more he breathed, as he released the held energy of his body and soul. Sometime, between the timeless tears, he began *breathing*. And in a moment or year, the breath of Seth's soulful tears broke through the layers of the held potential energy that lay deeply imbedded in the adipose tissues of his suffocated being. With time, he began to soulfully feel and know that he was literally too much energy, not too little. He realized that he simply did not know how to spin the power that he was *being*.

And in one random less than a second, Seth began to *feel* that he was enough. Somehow, the focused energetic tenacity of his soulful tears melted ignorance and rained gratitude. He felt his breath and being more and more as he unraveled the countless layers of his self- inflicted prison. Suddenly, eventually, he discovered his center inertia, and gained the innate awareness to feed himself from the inside out instead of the outside in. He became his own hero. He soulfully chose his own energetic *being*. Seth created a reality of freedom from the heavy weight of suffocation.

Now, as he releases himself into *being*, Seth alters his world with his infectious energy. He cries laughter. Sometimes, people even say that Seth is "a little too much", and he quietly smiles, knowing that he is just enough. He still loves a good video game, but when his right foot starts tapping, Seth heads for the kitchen, takes out the garbage, smiles at his mother, and runs outside to play with his friends.

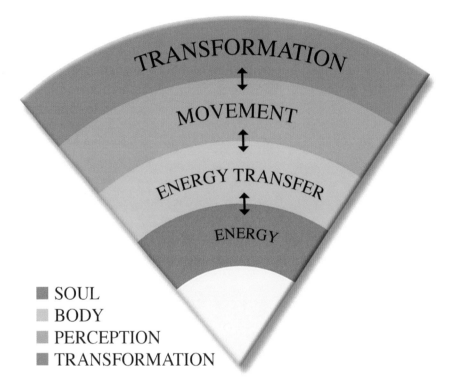

# The Soul

The soul's access to universal energy is the core inertia that spins us. Energy in the soulful sense is ever present, expansive, and endless. As a part of the expanding universe however defined; innately our souls possess access to all transformative energetic power. Our *beings*, both physically and spiritually are ultimately driven by universal energy. The souls' capacity and ability to *be* in, feel, and utilize this universal energy determines our soulful nergetic power to manifest and transform our *being*, and the resulting casual energy released from this transformation.

There is no lack of energy in the universe; in fact; there is more than enough for every soul to be forever energetically blissful in every moment. Energy *is*. It is neither created nor destroyed. It merely transforms. The soulful "energetic drain" that we often experience as humans *being* is not a result of actual "lack of energy'; rather the soul's inability to access it.  Our soulful knowing of how much and what type of energy is available to us determines how much and what type of energy we can access.

The amount of "energy we soulfully know and feel" is available to us is actually the amount of energy we have, as soulful intention is ultimately causal.  If we feel and know there is sufficient energy to manifest soulful intention, there is. If we feel and know that there is not sufficient energy to manifest soulful intention, the energy is not available to us.

We can only manifest from the raw soulful energy that we are. As we manifest, we energetically recreate ourselves. Intention must manifest through the energy of our *being*. If we are energetically less; we manifest from less. If we are energetically more; we manifest from more.

Manifestation itself releases energy. If we manifest from less soulful energetic power, we release less energy. If we manifest from more soulful energetic power, we release more energy.

The universal laws of energetic attraction dictate that energy attracts like energy, in amount and type. We attract what we are. If we are soulfully manifesting from less energetic power, we radiate less energy, and attract less energetic power. If we are soulfully manifesting from more energetic power, we radiate more energy, and attract more energetic power. If we manifest from held potential energy, we manifest held potential energy. If we manifest from the flow of kinetic energy, we manifest more flow of kinetic energy.

We attract how we are *being*. If we soulfully feel and be in "bad or negative energy", we attract hate, sadness, anger, helplessness, greed and despair. If we soulfully feel and be in "good or positive energy", we attract kindness, gratitude, truth, and the pure universal energy of love.

Although these all of these "spiritual laws of energy" have been known to be scientific and spiritual universal truths for some time, most humans still have great difficulty accessing the power of this knowledge. In fact, many of us would rather live and be in denial of our own soulful power than accept the responsibility that comes with the true acceptance of it.

If we be and exist in the truth that ultimately, individually and collectively, we decide the energy we access, the energy we are, and the energy we create; we then, in every given moment are responsible for our intentions, our physical *being*, our actions, our lives, and the resulting energy that we release out to create our world. If we decide and choose the energy we are, the energy we create, and the energy we attract, the world no longer happens to us because we create it. We have no one to blame but ourselves.

For many, the fear of this reality of accountability outweighs the benefits of a conscious soulfully chosen experience of *being* in this world. This fear and denial of soulful energetic power not only limits our access to universal energies; it causes energetic blocks in the breath, physical body, nervous system and mind. These held blocks of potential energy, in turn, further hinder transformative energetic access.

Fortunately and unfortunately, regardless of our energetic awareness and power of soulful intention, because we are energy, we are energetically creating our world and ourselves anyway; consciously and subconsciously. Whatever energy we release in *being*, we literally live in and with, individually and collectively. If the power of our own soulful center inertia is weakened or falters, by default, we are at the mercy of all energetic influences around us. It then becomes difficult for us to soulfully choose the energy that we are, or the energetic world in which we live.

Our access to the power of soulful energy is constantly influenced not only by our own state of *being*, but also by the energetic pull of world collective energy. If we are not soulfully spinning ourselves and grounding with our own inertia, the energy of the *beings* and world around us will spin us for us. Quite often we spiral soulfully out of control; victims to the energy of others and of the pull of the universe. We are left energetically imbalanced as our lives fling us in one direction and then another, leaving us nervous, disoriented, dull, and physically, mentally, and emotionally exhausted.

The balance of our own soulful energy and the soulful energy of other is a constant challenge of the human condition. As energetic *beings*, we crave to connect and merge with other souls, to connect with all that is of universal energy. Our relationships with loved ones, family, friends, and coworkers are moment-to-moment opportunities to test our own ability to ground and connect with our own soulful center inertia while engaging in the energies beyond self. As we consciously or subconsciously share and intermingle with the energy of other, we engage and spin an energetic dance of connection, balance and power. These energetic relationships of our souls with the souls of other either empower us and feed our own inertia, or sap us energetically until we cease to spin.

Fortunately, we exist as souls in meat-suits, and in every less than a second we have the opportunity to use the tools and power of the physical body to replenish and stabilize the energy of the soul. Just as soulful energy connects through the breath to the body and creates our physical *being*, the release of physical energy through the breath, nervous system, and body allows us to fall into center access and feed the inertia of the soul. As we feed the soulful sense through our breath and nervous system, it feels and becomes stronger energetically. The soul is then able to spin and maintain center energy regardless of the chaos that surrounds it.

Ultimately, energetic power lies in the simple decision to be in and access universal energy through the soul, and with intention, manifest it through the breath, the body and nervous system. Ultimately, we can choose to *be* in our positive energetic power in any given moment. We always have access to this power. We *are* this power. If we choose to feel and *be* in unlimited positive energies, we can, through breath and intention, transform our *being*. Through our energetic release, we transform our world.

*So take a moment or a year to notice the energy of your soul.*

Do you feel powerful in your intentions?

Do you feel you are and have enough?

Do you gain or lose energy from what you manifest?

Are you constantly energized, or physically tired or depressed?

Are you often bored or listless?

Do you feel scattered?

Do you need to rest often?

Do you have extraneous energy?

Are you physically and emotionally tense?

Are you physically or emotionally disengaged?

What type of energy do you attract?

# The Body

As humans *being*, energetically we can *only* be from what we are. We are the energy we recreate. Every less than a second we breathe and release into physical and soulful energies in constant instantaneous transformation. The way in which we manifest and transfer these energies through the physical systems is causal in our ability to manifest, *be*, and live in desired soulful intention.

The physical body is the energetic manifestation of the soul. As the soul moves through the breath and manifests itself in and through the body we create the energy of our physical and emotional *being*, our physical energetic reality. The ability to breathe and transfer oxygen through our systems literally creates the energy that creates us. How we access and transfer this energy through the physical systems dictates how much energetic power and choice is available to us. This resulting energetic power and choice creates and transforms our *being*.

Imagine for a moment, the physical body as a spinning top. The expansion of oxygen and soulful possibility into the body in inhalation creates its mass, the body or top as matter or potential energy. The power of release of exhalation into center manifests the energetic inertia that spins the nervous system and creates the energy of our *being* or spinning top. How we energetically expand and release into this center dictates how we spin: either in center in power, or off center in wobble and weakness.

A "real' top wobbles and falls lifeless to the ground when its energetic power, inertia or center is compromised, and then begs for someone to spin it. Humans *being*, when compromised, energetically, cling desperately to the mass of their bodies, and then beg, pull, and hold energy from the outside in to create and uphold *being*. The physical manifestation of the energetic body now stands upright by the conflicting force of opposing internal and external energies, rather than the free energetic spin of release. While as humans *being* we might appear superficially to be functioning, energetic, and stable; a second glance will reveal us as tortured souls crying to spin free from the prison of energetically held bodies and minds.

As the body, emotions, and mind are held, the expansion and release of the breath is further compromised. Unable to access universal energy, ground, manifest, and spin freely from center, we now beg the surrounding energies of the world to stabilize and spin us. *Being* is no longer soulful choice.

In a perfect energetic reality, everything we breathe and experience flows purely into us, through us, and out of us without complication. Like a spinning top, *being* is effortlessly energetically grounded into the earth. Ideally, our nervous system is in release, open, and able to move any amount or type of energies through the body in a very free manner.

However, as humans *being*, we all experience some form of energetic holding patterns that manifest themselves as held energy and tension in the physical body. Whatever the cause, physical or emotional stress, inefficient breath or movement patterning, environment, boredom, or simply life itself, the body often finds itself a refuge for stray energy. Extraneous, misplaced, or compensatory energy literally clogs the nervous system and induces imbalance in the bodies' systems. This held potential energy causes pain, anxiety, depression, mental illness, disease, fatigue, muscle imbalance and ineffective movement patterning.

As the physical body becomes weakened, energetic flow is further compromised, and these energetic blocks begin to multiply and feast upon each other. Left unidentified or unattended, these bundles of extraneous energy literally leave the human body trapped feeling and *being* held negative energy. The negative energy of the body's blocks and holding patterns conflicts with the positive energy flow of soulful intention. Manifestation of soulful energy into *being* is compromised.

The simple awareness of cause and type of energetic holding and how it manifests itself in the body is instrumental in unwrapping and releasing the kinetic energetic flow. The more we are able to understand and subconsciously/sometimes consciously feel the different energetic flows of the body, the greater capacity we have to release energetic holding patterns.

Energy of the human body is defined in many forms. In the eastern medical and yogic systems, energy is explained as Shakti, Prana, Kundalini, psycho energetic subtle bodies, or chi, to name a few. Western systems define energies of the physical body through the terminologies of neurological electricity, calories and oxygen exchange. Energy of the human body, regardless of form, is causal of itself and all other "types" of physical energies. Ultimately, energy is energy, and the body is created from it as the body manifests it.

For purposes of simplicity in an extremely complex subject matter of types, forms and abilities of energy, we will refer to the energy of the body in two forms; physical energy or tangible measurable energy, and psycho energetic or subtle energy, the energy of emotion and soul. While these two basic energetic forms are ultimately comprised of universal energy and therefore causal of each other and synergistic, they each manifest themselves and transfer through the body in their own unique fashion.

Although intricately complex, in basic principle the manifestation, movement, and transfer of physical energy in the body is really somewhat simplistic. As humans being, we are alive because we breathe. The energy we create as we breathe in o2-Co2 exchange feeds the nervous system. The raw energy of the breath is eventually through process manifested as electrical energy by the nervous system. The nervous system controls how we move energy through the body to create ourselves and manifest more energy. Because we breathe and manifest ourselves, we move, we eat and drink. We then create chemical energy and heat from our movement and caloric intake of potential energy. This allows us to physically *be*, grow, transform, and live.

All of this living and *being* happens as a result of the *if*, the *how*, and the *why* of the breath. In the physical body, the release into the breath, and the way in which intention in the breath finds and engages in center, grounds, and manifests the electrical energy of the nervous system dictates *how* and *what* energy moves through us to create us, and our physical energetic presence in the world.

Because we breathe, the central nervous system, which consists of the brain and spinal chord, manifests electrical energy that travels through the peripheral nervous system and out into all areas of the body. This electrical energy stimulates the chemical energy that runs our bodies' systems, from the skeletal muscular system to the organ systems. The sensory nervous system then sends messages back from the body's systems to the central nervous system and tells it how the body is energetically *being* in that less than a second. However the central nervous system subconsciously and sometimes consciously perceives the state of the body's energy determines how we take our next breath, and thus where and how the energy travels.

**Breath and energy transfer are causal of each other.**

If we are energetically in holding, the breath becomes held.

If we are energetically in release, the breath flows freely.

If the breath is held, we are energetically in holding.

If the breath flows freely in release, energetic pathways are clear.

As one might imagine, the energetic pathways of the nervous system are extremely intricate, both electrically and chemically, and the possibilities for misfiring, misinformation, and disconnection are plentiful. When the nervous system is challenged, either over stimulated, under stimulated or clogged, the extraneous energy caused by inefficiency in energy transfer leaves pockets of electric tension and chemical waste in the tissues of the body. These pockets of energetic waste form literal energy blocks in the body.

When the nervous system and tissues of the body are blocked, this held energy compromises the freedom of expansion and release in the breath. When the breath is compromised, the nervous system is further compromised, and this instability feeds upon itself. Subconsciously and sometimes consciously, we no longer move from center energy. We wobble precariously off center, even though our cognitive perceptive sense may tell us that everything is fine because we still can hold on and somehow pull in enough energy to stand up and spin.

Energetic holding patterns are most easily identified in the skeletal muscular system. The human skeleton, muscles, and connective tissues are literally designed to move energetically from the inside out. Just as the universe expands and a top spins, the body operates most efficiently when it is moving from a grounded stable center axis, regardless of what movement is required.

In an energetically balanced skeleton, the pelvis is stabilized by engaged central energy. This centered energy allows the deep subconscious of the central nervous system to fire the muscles and tissues of stabilization that ground, support and align the skeleton. The external musculature fires from a state of release and moves with ease as it is supported by the subconscious power and safety of stable center energy and alignment. The *kinesthetic chain*, or order and neurological firing of muscle fibers and muscle groups, functions freely and efficiently through the pathways of an aligned skeleton and open nervous system. This allows the entire body to engage in movement and life with ease.

When center energy fails, the skeletal system is most often the first to know, consciously or subconsciously. The moment the breath fails to release into center and flow freely, the neurological system holds, and the grounding and movement from center energy out is compromised. The body literally falls out of alignment as the medial energy is lost. The stabilizers fail to stabilize, and the external musculature fires and holds in fear and imbalance as the brain commands it to "hold on and stand up".

As the musculature holds from the outside in, center energy is further diminished. This lack of center energy blocks the efficiency of firing in the kinesthetic chain causing further holding, instability, and inefficient movement patterning in the skeletal system. This stress of imbalance and held skeletal energy is most often the cause of inexplicable aching hips, tight shoulders, stiff necks, low back pain, and acute injury or arthritis due to muscle imbalance and inefficient kinesthetic patterning.

Energetic holding in the skeletal muscular system not only causes difficulty in stabilization and movement. As the body holds from the outside in, compromised alignment and toxins accumulated in the skeletal system affect the organ systems as well. When the neurological system is stressed and inefficient, the chemical energy of the body becomes imbalanced. This compromises the function of the hormonal system, immune system, and digestive system, circulatory system, respiratory system, and often creates more holding patterns in the skeletal system. Held physical energy, whether chemical or electric, and inefficient energy transfer is causal in high blood pressure, digestive issues, fertility issues, cancer, respiratory issues and disease. As we become weakened by physical illness and pain, we feel bad, and often begin to *be* in and emit, and attract negative energy. This further compromises our physical energetic state of *being*.

How we feel emotionally, our psycho energetic state of *being*, and how we transfer these subtle energies through the body, greatly affect our physical *being* and our access to transformative energetic power. As the soulful sense is ultimately causal, this emotional energetic power must consciously and subconsciously align with soulful intention, and move freely through the emotional feeling sense of the physical *being*. Whatever we feel and are energetically in the subtle body is a causal factor in the ultimate energy of our *being*.

While this psycho energetic energy has until recently been difficult to define or measure in western physical terms of electricity or chemical energy, the eastern medical systems have successfully utilized the subtle energetic systems of the body to influence and cause transformative change in the body for longer than the knowledge of western tangible energy has been alive. Thankfully, in the past decade due to the advances in science and technology, we are now literally able to see how our thoughts, soulful intentions, emotions, and feelings have causal affect on the physical energetic systems of the body. We now know that how we are *being* in the psycho energetic system greatly influences and often ultimately controls the physical energy of the human body.

Every conscious or subconscious emotional feeling or soulful intention that is experienced in humans *being* is associated with the breath. We feel and move soulful intention through us because we breathe, and our feelings and soulful intentions are deeply connected to our breathing patterns. Because we are "breathing energy" through every moment of our life experience, every feeling, experience, or emotion has an associated breathing pattern that resides in the subconscious energetic system.

The feeling of "happy" stimulates the breath a certain manner, the feeling of "fear or sadness" triggers the breath in another. Just as we are subconsciously wired to breathe a certain way in "fight or flight", we are subconsciously wired to breathe how we are *being* in the subtle body in any given breath. Our energetic feeling and subconscious energetic knowing tell the body how to breathe, unless we consciously soulfully tell it otherwise. As we know, the breath controls the nervous system that controls the physical energetic flow of the body. This complex circular synergistic dance of cause and effect of the psycho energetic system, the breath and the physical energetic system creates the ultimate energy that the human *being* experiences and releases.

Physical issues in the body are, therefore, quite often manifestations of psycho energetic blockage. Holding patterns and misplaced energy of the psycho energetic systems literally find a home in the tissues and systems of physical energy.

For example, in the psycho energetic Chakra System, stress, sadness, loneliness, and anger, all a result of heart chakra issues, are quite often apparent in those humans who experience high blood pressure, heart disease, asthma, anxiety, thoracic spine, shoulder, wrist, or carpal issues. Those *beings* with third chakra or "power and manifestation issues" often manifest ulcers, digestive issues, and cancers of the stomach and colon. Security and emotional issues of the first and second chakra often cause inexplicable low back and hip pain, and wreak havoc on sexual energies, fertility, and the reproductive and elimination systems.

Mirroring the tangible energy of the skeletal system, energy of the psycho energetic systems also grounds and travels from the base of the pelvis, through the spine and out into the extremities. The root of all emotive energy, the "Muladhara" or root chakra lives at the base of the pelvis, and is causal for the balance of all other subtle energies. Just as the pelvis centers energy and creates the grounding and stability of the medial line in the physical energetic systems, the root chakra is the energetic center and stabilizer of the entire psycho energetic system. Regardless of where manifested energy may be blocked in the psycho-energetic systems, the root chakra, by default, is energetically causal of the "problem", and necessary in solution.

In the root chakra lives our soulful purpose and right to be on this earth, our connection and security in the physical body and world. A stable connected, grounded, fearless root chakra allows the human *being* to energetically move soulful intention confidently through the entire psycho-energetic system and body in balanced emotion, manifestive power, love, creativity, mindfulness and intuitive *being*.

Just as an unstable pelvic energy causes the skeletal system to hold in fear, lack of stability and grounding in the root chakra energies causes the psycho energetic system to hold in fear. This basis of fear moves energetic intention through the psycho energetic body and subtle body systems in imbalanced emotion, compromised power, tainted love, stifled creativity, clouded perception, and dampened intuitive access.

Like its physical energetic counterpart, imbalance in the energy flow of the psycho energetic systems causes pockets of held energy. These held emotive tensions manifest as emotional blocks in specific areas of the subtle body. Often unrecognized by the perceptive sense, barriers in the emotional structure and subtle body may for years exist in the body unnoticed, and create inefficient movement patterning and energy flow in the psycho energetic system. These subconscious emotive blocks often leave the human *being* wondering why he or she "just is or feels" a certain way, and is at a loss to "get past it". In extreme cases of psycho energetic misfire, barriers, and imbalance, all access to conscious or sub conscious emotive feeling in a specific area may be denied. The human *being* is crippled by blocked psycho energy, and left entirely unaware that any emotional issues exist at all.

The blocked and misplaced energies of the psycho energetic system are not only causal in the subtle body; they cause holding and imbalance in the correlating physical systems of the body. As the emotional energy alters breathing patterning and energy transfer through the nervous system, the physical systems are affected. Regardless of origin of cause, energy is energy, and holding is holding. The synergistic energetic cycle continues.

Fortunately, as humans *being*, we are alive because we breathe. Ultimately, the breath consciously or sub consciously controls all of the energy of the body, regardless of type, and our energy exists in us because the breath moves it through us.

Through the gifts of the breath and body, we have many ways to access and create transformative energy. If we listen to the *if*, *how*, and *why* of the breath, we have access to energetic change. This simple gift of breathing allows us to investigate any energetic imbalances in our physical or emotional being. Consciously, through the soulful intention of our inhale, exhale and transfer of energy, we can release the nervous system, and free the blocks and barriers that clog our energetic systems.

Because of the synergy that exists between the physical energies and subtle energies of the body, we are able to release mental and emotional blocks through the physical energy systems of the body, and blocks of the physical systems through the release of psycho energetic stress and holding patterns. If we choose to focus our soulful intention through the breath to release our holding patterns, and create unobstructed energetic flow in all of our systems of *being*, the possibilities to manifest transformation in our physical bodies, our lives, and our world are endless.

*So take a moment or a year to notice the energy of your human being.*

Are you often lethargic, lack motivation, or can't quite seem to get things done?

Are you "high strung"?

Do you exercise obsessively?

Are you inactive?

Are you hyperactive?

Are you moody or uncomfortable in your body?

Are you often bored?

Do you "work hard" and "get nowhere"?

Do you experience inexplicable tension, back pain, neck pain, fibromyalgia, or carpal tunnel syndrome?

Are you endlessly tired?

Are you obese or underweight?

Do you have eating disorders?

Do you have cancer, heart or circulatory issues, digestive issues, migraines, or T.M.J.?

Do you experience insomnia, anxiety, attention deficit disorder, or depression?

Do you have arthritis or chronic joint pain?

Do you have issues with your feet, hands, or toes?

# Perception

As the world spins, we stand, move, and *be*, consciously unaware that the earth is spinning until a cognitive stimulus brings it to our attention. As humans *being*, we spin through our lives on a spinning world like tops, and rarely do we think about or realize how and why we are energetically spinning; we simply spin. We do not often consciously perceive about the energy of our *being*, or that we are *being*, we simply *be*.

Although the human psyche, ego, and mind like to think that they are consciously cognitively perceptively aware and causal of everything, in reality, most of our perception is born in the subconscious. Most often, our neurological systems subconsciously perceive and decide what and how energy is moving through the body, and rarely does this information ever reach conscious or cognitive perception.

If and when this subconscious energetic decision does actually in awareness meet the cognitive mind for review, usually the nervous system has already subconsciously told the mind "how it is, what is possible, how it is going to be". The causal energy of the subconscious has often already acted on its own, leaving the cognitive mind wondering "why I just thought that" or "why I keep doing that ". Our subconscious feeling and knowing, once again, dictate our transformative reality. We exist and *be* in transformative choice when soulful intention is energetically perceived by the subconscious energetic systems as possibility, and granted access to move through the human energetic systems.

As humans *being*, literally we can only perceive from where we are and how we transfer energy through our nervous systems. Whatever we *are being* energetically is our lens of perception. Because the subconscious energy and energetic patterning of the neurological system is causal in what the conscious cognitive mind perceives and thinks, blocks in soulful energetic access or barriers in the physical energetic and psycho energetic systems can cause both subconscious and cognitive perception to become limited and skewed.

Quite often, years after an injury or trauma to a human *being* has occurred, the subconscious nervous system perceives and acts out in pain, holding, or "fight or flight" even though the *being*'s cognitive perception knows that presently nothing is wrong. For example, frequently in cases of spinal injury and trauma, long after the injury is healed and danger is no longer present, subconscious energetic holding and skewed neurological patterning trigger pain receptors and muscle contractors to fire and protect the spine. This creates inexplicable back spasm and chronic pain in an area that has "already healed". These spasms feed upon themselves creating more blocked energy and holding patterns until subconscious and cognitive perception now "think" there is a problem…. so there is. Unless energetic intervention is practiced, the effected human *being* will go on endlessly energetically knowing and experiencing that back pain is simply "how it is." The "bad energy" of back pain now becomes the perceptive energetic norm of the *being*. This normal "bad energy" then attracts "bad energy" and propagates itself. The simple subconscious energetic holding and misfire of perceived back pain finds the human *being* mummified in a body and life wound from countless threads of energetic misperception.

Often in the case of post-traumatic stress disorder or anxiety, sub conscious blocks and neurological triggers are deeply embedded in the physical and psycho energetic systems. Random external stimuli cause the subconscious nervous system to fire energetic signals of fear and panic, and the physical body finds itself suddenly in a "fight or flight" situation without any cognitive knowledge of how it all happened. By the time cognitive perception sets in and understands why, it is already to late to reverse the energetic chaos. This energetic chaos, in turn, causes more trauma and energetic blockage. Without intervention, the pattern feeds upon itself. Fear becomes embedded in the energy of *being*. Transformation is then perceived and becomes complicated and difficult.

While energetic perception issues are obviously apparent in extreme cases of pain and trauma, as humans *being* we all experience subconscious perceptive pockets and patterns of energetic holding and misfire. We are all subject to limited and skewed perceptions that stifle transformative energetic flow.

Every moment of life carries with it an energy that passes through the human systems. Sometimes this energy flows freely through, and sometimes it doesn't. Trauma or bliss, the backdrop of energetic patterning created by our life experience molds all of our perceptions. As we engage in the present, we perceive through the energetic patterning and pathways of our past, unless we clear and recreate them from the inside out.

Try as we might to "change our mindset" and "alter our perception"; our "mindset" only treats the momentary symptom of perceptive issue. We can tell ourselves to "see things differently and be differently" but only true change in our energetic *being* can heal the root cause of "how we see and be". Until we release the blockage in our energetic systems and change the energy that we *are* and the energy we attract, ultimately, we will keep feeling, *being*, and perceiving in the same way.

While with "mindset" we may be able to cognitively create some change in our perceptions with our calculated momentary actions and thoughts, the physical and psycho-energetic energy and feelings that drive thought, action, and perception will remain unaltered. We tell ourselves and cognitively "perceive" we are seeing and *being* differently when in actuality, the true image remains unchanged through the same old lens of the subconscious. We will feel and *be* the same even though our behavior and cognitive perception of it is momentarily altered. Victims of self- inflicted cloudy perception; we fool ourselves into thinking that desired perceptive transformation has occurred, and then wonder why this doesn't ultimately change us or make us feel or act any differently.

Although the energetic complexities of the nervous system may seem to deem transformative change and clarity of perception to be impossibility, a clear window of perception is readily available to us with every breath we take. The breath controls the nervous system that controls the energetic flow of our *being*. As we expand energetic possibility with inhalation and release our physical and psycho-energetic energetic pathways with exhalation, we clear our nervous system and transform our perceptive lens. Clear energetic pathways offer clear perception, both conscious and subconscious. As we energetically perceive in truth, we attract the energy of truth. As we attract truth, we become the energy of truth. As we are *being* truth, we are centered from truth. The energy of soulful intention now grounds and spins freely through us from the inside out, and energetic perception becomes the mirror of the soul.

*So take a moment or a year to notice the energy of your perception.*

Do you notice what you feel like when you think or perceive?

Do you notice the quantity and type of energy surrounding you and your perceptions?

Do you perceive through a positive or negative energetic lens?

Do you hold on and perceive through past experiences even though you want to let go and see things differently?

Can you tap into the energetic feeling of you, and allow your thoughts and cognition to wash over and through you?

Are you constantly feeling the necessity to form a concrete answer?

Do you breathe, feel, and then make a perceptive choice?

Do negative feelings wreck your day?

Do you hold your breath and talk yourself into seeing things in a positive light?

Do you physically hold perception or exhale release into it?

Do you feel and understand the energy you emit?

# Transformation

Energy itself, like life, is in a constant instantaneous state of transformation. Energy is raw transformation waiting to be spun.

The gift of the human condition is that *we* choose. *I and We* choose the energy that we are, the energy we spin, and the energy we manifest. With every breath, we transform our *being* and our world.

Energy itself becomes transformative choice in that less than a second when desired soulful intention is embraced by the breath, nervous system and perception, and flows freely through our human to soulfully choose our *being*. This transformative energy of *being* is causal, and in that less than a second, *being* soulfully transforms our world.

# Being

*" 'Oh Eleph-ant!" cried Baby Ant. . . .*
*"Behold the beautiful blue sky!'*
*'What sky?' retorted Eleph-ant.*
*'I can't see it! I hear only the sounds of the jungle!'*
*'Silly Eleph-ant,' Baby Ant replied. 'I can't see it either. . . but I can feel it!...*
*You hear what?'*
*Eleph-ant was quite annoyed.*
*'Just go back to the place that you come from!' he spouted.*
*'I am here' Baby Ant replied."*

Somehow, somewhere in the great oceans of the universe, a tiny droplet ebbs and flows with the tide. She dives to the depths and rises to the surface with countless others, spinning endlessly in and through the timeless current until one moment or year she is pulled towards the distant shore. The surge of the tide becomes stronger and stronger as her wave of countless droplets swells towards the break.

Tiny droplet is tossed and tumbled, stretched and twisted to the brink of explosion as she fights to ride the wave towards her chosen destination. In sudden endlessness, her wave swells and morphs until the timeless flow finally breaks it. Somewhere, somehow, in less than a second, her reality is shattered.

Tiny droplet wakes to find her self floating in the sparkling spray, expanding and opening towards the infinite sky. She is herself, yet in form somehow different, her *being* lighter and fluffier than ever before. She feels more sky than wave. She expands and drifts with the great floating wind, filling herself with fluffiness to her soul's content until quite instantaneously; her fullness condenses and collapses into small and heavy.

The sky no longer holds her, and she plummets purposefully downward, a diamond sparkle in timeless motion. In that moment or year, with eyes wide open, droplet tumbles blindly and releases into chosen destiny.

She explodes on impact. She becomes more of herself, tiny fragments of her former self; yet somehow, a droplet all the same. Stronger, fuller, and lighter, the essence of her *being* grounds. Particles of her broken gem begin to gather and spiral upwards. She ascends and spins with her swirling tide until miraculously, in less than a second she winds herself into herself only to spin again. Pure center inertia releases her outward into *being* as she rolls into a soft bed of radiant purple velvet.

The sky rains waves of diamonds.

Such is all *being*: The droplet and the wave in simultaneity; timeless possibility swimming through diamond shattered flowers that spin a bed of iridescent purple velvet for droplets of the soul.

*Being* causing *being* in constant instantaneous transformation.

# Phillip Grey Smith

Phillip Grey Smith was an amazing human being; not because of what he did, but because of how he was. A child born into a poor farming family of alcoholics, he somehow managed through the years to manifest himself into a successful lawyer, loving husband, father, philanthropist, and most importantly, expert gardener. His physical life spanned a century allowing him to live through two world wars, the great depression, Vietnam, and numerous presidents and civil rights policies. He experienced prohibition, the invention of the automobile, the telephone, the typewriter, and the computer.  A simple conversation with the man was akin to time travel through a detailed history book. In the course of his lifetime he expanded into countless innovations and new ideas of thought. And yet, the wealth of worldly stories, knowledge, wisdom, and material manifestation he created as a human *being* were not the things remembered about him on the day of his death. Anyone who really knew Phillip Grey Smith knew that the most amazing thing about him was the way he ate his eggs at breakfast.

He awoke like a coiled spring at exactly seven o'clock every morning. Without fail, he practiced twenty minutes of calisthenics and stretching, and prepared himself for the day. This in itself was no easy task. The last thirty- five years of his life, his beloved wife Edith was an invalid. Phillip was not only responsible to prepare himself for a long day at the office; he was the main caregiver for his wife, and thus woke and prepared her for the day as well.

 Task briskly yet calmly accomplished, he would head down the spiral staircase to the kitchen and begin the breakfast preparation. The menu rarely varied aside from the pancakes served on Sundays. Breakfast always began with fresh squeezed orange juice, and continued on with soft-boiled eggs and whole-wheat toast. Before he ate his own meal, he would respond to the cry of "Yoo Whooo…Phil!" that rang down the stairwell, and take a serving of the morning feast up to his beloved wife.

As a child visiting my grandfather, and later on as a young adult temporarily living in his house, this clattering of china and my grandmother's cries awakened me. The smell of fresh toast and coffee would eventually lure me out of the warm feather bed and down the stairs to the sunny breakfast nook that overlooked the endless garden. This was the place where the magic happened. This was where Phillip Grey Smith ate his breakfast.

 As a young girl, I didn't notice the marvel of it so much. I only took in the fact that my grandfather always sat still in the same chair, and calmly ate his breakfast while the chaos of two parents and three grandchildren buzzed frantically around him shouting, clanking, banging, and occasionally spilling juice and breaking dishes. I always wondered how he sliced his egg perfectly in half in its eggcup, and managed to scoop out all the delicious contents without a trace of shell. I remember, when I was really little, asking him how he did that a few times; how he could perfectly and meticulously get all of the beautiful egg out of the shell every time with no breakage. He would smile and calmly explain the process to me, and I would clumsily try to imitate it. I never did master the soft-boiled egg excavation; and yet, as I grew older, I didn't ask him how he did it anymore. I would watch him in wonderment for a moment; and then most often, I became involved with my own egg and left him unnoticed.  It was not that I didn't want to learn or that he was tuned out or unavailable. I still wondered how he did it, and he was always eager and ready to engage with his grandchild. I simply didn't want to disturb him. He seemed so peaceful sitting there eating his egg and reading his paper. There was an uncanny air of grace about him. It was much more enjoyable to just eat my own egg and watch him eat his. There was something was quite beautiful about it.

Like clockwork, somewhere around the last bite of his toast, the alarm from upstairs would cry "Yooo- Whoooo Phil!" My grandfather would calmly smile. Without a trace of annoyance, he would sip his last sip of coffee, take his dishes to the kitchen, and head up the stairs to tend to the needs of his wife. Some time after that, he quietly slipped out the back door and disappeared to his office for a full day of work.

It wasn't until I was much older that I began to take in much more of who Phillip Grey Smith was as a human *being*. Like many young adults in their early twenties, I began to acknowledge the richness of my grandfather's life and accomplishments, and notice as well that he was no saint. I recognized his stubbornness and need to be right. I saw how he could instantaneously flash a split second of evil eye, and manipulate his fellow humans into guilt. I saw how his highly intelligent mind could calculate to a fault. Yet despite all his apparent misgivings, he still had a way of *being* in breakfast that was beyond explanation.

As a rock star (at least in my own mind), at the age of twenty-two, I lived at my grandfather's house for an extended period of time. I was very busy at the time, working night and day in the recording studio, and trying desperately to live up to the legend in my own mind. I rarely noticed anything beyond the frantic pace and chaotic realm of my own self-inflicted reality. And yet, when Phillip Grey Smith sat down to his breakfast, time stood still.

I would stand by the toaster, impatiently waiting for my toast, and suddenly become mesmerized by the grace of my grandfather as he consciously exhaled and lowered his ninety-year-old bones delicately into his chair. He unfolded his napkin, placed it on his lap, and paused for a split second to gaze out at the garden. He smiled. Then slowly and meticulously he arranged his newspaper, took a sip of coffee, reached for his knife, and began that incredible, seemingly unattainable 'tap, tap, tap" on his eggshell that began the unearthly manifestation of the perfectly procured spoonful of soft-boiled egg. "How did he do that?" I was awed. "How did he calmly engage in every last bit of the moment when the constant chaos of life echoed frantically off the walls of the breakfast nook? How did he smile at the weeds in the garden that needed pulling and marvel at the flowers? How did he know just where and how hard to tap the eggshell to get the perfect bite? How did he quietly relish reading his paper when he had a full day of work ahead, and bills to be paid, and dinner to be made? How did he endlessly feel and respond with love to the relentless reverberation of my grandmother's screams? How did he *do* that?"

Somehow, regardless of the reality of the moment, in every less than a second he was able to expand in awareness of the world around him as he released grounded soulful intention through his *being* and manifested the perfect amount and type of energy to radiate grace. "How could he *be* like that? How did he, in every less than a second, *be* in grace?"

As of this moment, I am still in awe. Through the years, with practice, I have come a bit closer to understanding the breakfast eating prowess of my grandfather, but by no means does the energy of my *being* radiate a particle of the graceful causal energy with which he moved through his life.

At his memorial celebration, there was brief mention of his entrepreneurial spirit, his highly esteemed law practice, his alumni contributions to Stanford

University, his great philanthropic garden party fundraisers, his family legacy, and his years of devotion to his wife. Mostly, however; the intimate meaningful conversations about his life revolved around his ability to constantly expand into new ideas and possibilities, his love for grounding his soulful intention by digging in the dirt, his gift for manifesting beautiful flowers, and of course, the endless energy of his loving *being*. Those who had the gift of really knowing Phillip Grey Smith simply discussed the amazing uncanny way that he ate his eggs at breakfast, and words became entirely unnecessary.

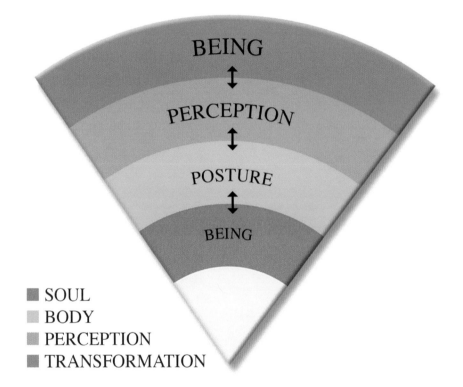

# The Soul

As humans *being*, we are the less than a second result of our journey through expansion, intention, and manifestation of energy. However the soul opens to the sea of possibility, chooses intention, engages in manifestation, and creates soulful energy, determines our soulful *being*; whatever *it* is that we draw through our physical body and out into world. How we are *being* in the soulful sense is the root of our reality, and is ultimately causal of all transformation that we choose and experience in the physical world. Our ability to connect with, *be* in, and transform the fabric of our soul determines our transformative possibility and choice.

While our life experiences, physical body, and breath and nervous system greatly affect our soulful sense of *being*, in the end, the soul decides how our being is. That subconscious feeling and knowing that we all experience as humans *being* is ultimately causal of itself. If we soulfully decide to breathe and release into our subconscious feeling and knowing, we have access to transform our patterns of soulful *being*. This release into soulful *being* is really the only thing in our life experience that we actually have the ability to control. Fortunately, it is the origin and cause of *being* in life.

Ironically, the human body, nervous system, perceptive sense and cognitive mind, when challenged will attempt to control, and do everything possible to lead our *being* away from soulful sensation. As the subconscious and conscious nervous system kick in and tell the body and cognitive mind to "gain control" of the situation at hand; they remove us energetically from our soulful power. Instead of diving into the soulful power that actually facilitates desired change, our frantic physical *being* often swims away from it and then blames itself and the world for creating undesired transformation. As we are *being* in a state of undesired transformation, we feel further removed from the soulful sense, and perceive that our "life" is weakening our soul. Ultimately, nothing can weaken the soul other than the soul itself, for the true power of humans' *being* lies deep within the cycle of soulful *being*. We must learn to swim beyond ourselves and *be* in a way that allows us to dive into the soul and embrace it.

We can use the tools of life experience and the physical body to empower our soulful sense of *being*. Years of hatha yoga practice and somatic therapies have proven that when we engage in the physical aspects of our *being*, we open ourselves to the wisdom and power of the soul. The more we tie into the breath and physical sensation, the more likely we are to connect with feeling and *be* soulful causality. The more connected we are with the *being* of our souls, the greater our ability is to *be* in transformative choice. If we can connect with our body and soul and be present in life experience, momentary life adventure becomes fuel for the soul.

The ability of humans *being* to *be* in soulful clarity and choice is key in transforming our realities, both individually and collectively. As soulful intentions pass through the vehicle of the physical body, they manifest the energy that creates our *being*. This *being* energetically bleeds out into the world in every less than a second and creates our individual and collective realities. Because energy attracts like energy, we are not only constantly instantaneously drawing more of what we soulfully are to us, we are creating our world to be more of what we soulfully are. Ultimately, only the power of the soul can transform the fabric of the universe.

> *So take a moment or a year to notice how you are being in the soulful sense....*

Can you feel how you are *being*?

Do you choose how you are *being*?

Are your actions in line with your intentions?

Does your *being* align with your soulful intentions?

Do you attract what you soulfully desire in your life?

Do you soulfully know who you desire to *be* in this world?

Are you who you soulfully desire to *be* in this world?

# The Body

We cannot *be* in physical reality, as we know it without the tool of the physical body. Our *being* in this world is the physical manifestation of our soul. The physical body is the vehicle that allows soulful energy to manifest as the physical energy of *being*. Although this physical state of *being* is ultimately created by the nature of the soul, our physical bodies are energetically causal of themselves. The state of the physical body influences our access to the soulful sense, and thus often dictates how the soul is in *being*.

In western culture we often perceive and cognitively believe that our physical structure and "health and well being" is a separate compartment, just one aspect of our lives. The truth is that our physical *being* really *is* our lives. Nothing "happens" to us or for us unless we breathe the soul through the body. The body is the container that manifests and feeds the soul out into the world, and like it or not; in the physical realm, the state of the body and our connection with it shape who and how we are *being*. The breath, body, and nervous system decide if and how we radiate our causal soulful energy out to create our world.

If we are soulfully separate from our physical *being* in any given less than a second, we are not truly *being* present in our transformative process. Disconnection between the soulful sense and physical body disallows soulful intention from moving through the physical systems. Manifested intention becomes random. Transformative choice is rendered impossibility. We no longer subconsciously or consciously feel and know how we are in *being*, therefore; we are unable to access or engage soulful choice.

Present, aware, or not, as humans *being*, we are constantly instantaneously transforming and transferring some form of energy through the body. We are constantly instantaneously happening, happening, happening, and the world is a different place because we are *being*. When physically disengaged from the power of the soul, we are unaware of our process of *being*. We are causal without awareness. We merely exist in our cognitive "idea" of our physical body and reality, as our unaware *being* chooses and creates our destiny. We may cognitively perceive or superficially feel that we are choosing our life path, but life is happening *to* us, not *from* us, or our soulful intention. Ideas are not causal. *Being is*.

Aware or unaware, once breathed into the realm of physical body, the soulful sense is at the mercy of the physical systems. Whatever and however the neurological, energetic, perceptive and physical structure of the human is *being* is the vehicle through which soulful intention must travel. If the physical body is open, released, engaged and able to manifest, soulful energy transfers freely through it and radiates in authentic *being*. If the physical systems and structures are closed, blocked and tense, soulful energy is compromised as it travels through the container of the body, and our intentional being is modified or incomplete. Ultimately, if the physical body is in a compromised state, we end up *being* and radiating a twisted, held, watered down version of our soulfully desired transformative self. Only the soulful intention to connect the breath with the soul and the ability to allow this soulful breath to open and release our physical *being* can reverse this compromised transformative state.

*Being* in the physical body is causal of the physical body. In the physical world, we can only *be* and transform from where and what we *are being*. The energy of our *being* is the state from which we transform. Because the energy of our physical *being* attracts like energy, unless we soulfully choose to intervene, we are constantly becoming more of what we physically are.

This is apparent in all challenges physical. If we are *being* in pain, we breathe, manifest, perceive and become the energy of pain; thus, we attract more pain. If we are *being* in obesity, we breathe, manifest, perceive, and become the energy of overweight; thus, we attract all that is "fat". If we are *being* in depression, we attract more sadness. If we are *being* in disease, we become more ill. These energetic patterns of *being* in the physical body feed upon themselves, and eventually cause the cognitive mind to believe "this is just how we are" or that we need to "fix ourselves""… and so we *be* that.

As we grapple in desperation to heal and change our bodies and minds through cognitive thoughts and actions, we once again, move our physical *being* farther away from the connection of the soulful sense. While positive affirming thoughts are helpful, even if we are thinking in "positive solutions" the underlying neurological assumption is that we need to "fix" a problem. If we are consciously or subconsciously neurologically and energetically "with problem", our physical *being* is "with problem", and attracts "with problem". What we really need to "do" is soulfully physically know and *be* without "problem". As we clear our breath and neurological systems to a neutral state, we are free to manifest transformative soulful intention through them and be and radiate chosen transformative change.

In the skeletal muscular system, for example; if we are tense or in pain due to injury or stress, we attract tension, especially to the affected area. As we are *being* in physical tension, our nervous system perceives tension and pain and is causal of it. When the affected area of the body experiences tension, not only does the muscular system draw tension to other areas of the body in compensatory kinesthetic patterning; the entire energy of the body becomes focused on tension, and the subconscious nervous system creates more of it. If we are *being* in tension, the more we exercise, stretch, and manually "do" and "work" to "fix" the tension, the more energy we draw to tension itself. This does not mean that traditional techniques such as strengthening musculature or "active release techniques" are not effective. It simply means that *how we are being* in the rehabilitative process greatly affects the long-term result of the chosen solution. Even if we are "thinking in positive solution", and intending to release, if we are subconsciously neurologically *being* in holding, the underlying perceived "problem" of the subconscious nervous system is still causal of tension and pain. Our rehabilitation program may give us some relief, but the root issues and cause of the pain and stiffness will be left unaddressed. Until we consciously and subconsciously soulfully release from "the problem of tension and pain" through the breath and nervous system, we will continue to manifest and be in tension and pain.

Ultimately, there is nothing to "fix" in the physical body, or the physical world, for that matter. We do not need to "fix" to transform. We need to soulfully choose to *be* differently from who and how we are *being*. The body, in whatever state, simply *is*, in every less than a second, the vehicle for the soul and breath to travel through. It is not good, bad, right, or wrong. The soul and the breath create it, and only the soul and the breath can truly transform it.

The physical body is not only causal of itself. In simple physical world terms, the world is a different place because I, you, and we are here. The reality of our bodies taking up physical and energetic space in our world is causal of our individual and collective reality.

Our physical impact in this world is blatantly apparent in our human creativity and environmental issues. As we recreate our human condition and world reality through our *being* in technology, bioengineering, scientific knowledge, and economic possibility; we transform our capacity of how we *be* in this world. This "advanced" state of physical *being* also recreates the ecological balance and energy of our planet that, in turn, directly affect our human systems. Toxins, genetically altered food, contaminated water sources, stressful environment, modern medicine, and over-population literally alter the physical cellular structure and energy of our humans *being*. As our humans *being* increase in number and space, the causal energy of our individual and collective physical *being* increases in power. Our *being* then has greater energetic impact on the universal reality that we create. As our physical and energetic influence transforms the fabric of the universe, we redefine our sea of possibilities.

While many humans love to blame economics, technological advancement, social issues, overpopulation, and religious views for the state of our world reality, the universal energetic truth is that the soulful energy released from our humans *being*, and the resulting cognitive thoughts and actions of our *being* cause our world to be what it *is*. We manifest what we *are*. We are all, as humans physically and energetically *being*, responsible for the reality of our world. *I* and *We* create *It*.

Our causal energy in the world is nothing more or less than the macrocosm of our individual physical and emotional *being*. Like our physical systems, ultimately we cannot "fix" our world through simple collective cognitive thought, political policy, and action. We must choose to *be* differently in our bodies and world, and *cause* the transformation of our reality. In every less than a second, the power of the soul and breath have the opportunity to clear the nervous system, physical body, perceptions, and cognition. In every less than a second, as humans physically *being*, we possess the power to transform our world.

*So take a moment or a year to notice how you are being in your physical body and world.*

Are you truly in touch with the state of your physical body?

Does your body feel connected with your soul and breath?

Do you feel the power to change your physical body?

Do you love and accept your body regardless of its present state?

Are you chronically or often ill?

Do you "feel old"?

Do you experience chronic pain or injury?

Are you aware of the tension and blocks in your body?

Do you look for someone or something else to relieve physical pain or discomfort?

Are you searching for someone other than yourself to "make you better"?

Do you use substance to check out or disconnect from your body and mind?

Can you release into physical pain or stress?

Do you possess the "physical energy" to carry out your soulful intentions?

Does your physical state of *being* interfere with your soulfully desired transformation?

What kind of energy do you emit and attract?

What and how does your physical *being* affect the world?

# Perception

*Being* in the perceptive sense is the less than a second awareness, observation, and interpretation of the energy released in manifestation. However and whatever we create from our process of expansion, intention, and manifestation of energy through the breath, physical body, and nervous system determines our template of perception. How we are *being* in perception is a result of our subconscious, conscious, and cognitive perception. Every less than an instant, the subconscious nervous system perceives, the conscious mind allows us to know that we are perceiving, and the cognitive mind tells us what our perception means. and what to *do* or *be* about it.

In *being*, conscious perception cannot exist without first moving through the subconscious perceptive system. All energy must move in some way through the energetic systems of the human *being* to be perceived. We are not constantly aware of how we are seeing, we simply see. We are unaware of how we are hearing, we simply hear. We are not often aware of why and how we are feeling, thinking and moving through life, we simply feel, think, and move through life.

Ironically, the energetic neurological process and perception of the subconscious is the causal root of all conscious perception and cognitive thought. Although we can alter our perceptions a bit if we are in the awareness of our conscious perception and cognitive thought, true transformative perception occurs on the subconscious level. We can change our perspective a bit by consciously cognitively deciding to change what we think or how we are in our lives, yet our perceptive process will remain unaltered. We will still *feel* and *be* in the same in our perceptive process even if our mind tells us we have expanded through it. Ultimately, to *be* in transformative perception, we must clear our subconscious perceptive pathways through the breath, nervous and energetic systems, and allow life to flow through us without bias or obstacle. As we clear our subconscious perceptive systems, expansive possibilities, soulful intention, and life experience, flow through our perceptive *being* in truth and non-judgment. As we perceive truth, we *be* in, radiate, and attract clarity. Perception itself becomes expandable.

Whatever and however the subconscious nervous system energetically perceives, the conscious mind deems to be true. We are only consciously aware of what moves through the process of the subconscious energetic systems.

Imagine, for example, that you perceive that there is "energy of giraffe" standing beside you. You saw it, heard it, felt it, smelled it, or just energetically "knew" that it was present. Somehow, the "energy of giraffe" entered your radar through your physical *being* and subconscious energetic system. You now consciously perceive your subconscious neurological and energetic systems' perception of "energy of giraffe". If you have consciously perceived "energy of giraffe" before, and your cognitive mind has defined it as "giraffe", you will consciously perceive that "energy of giraffe" is in actuality "giraffe." If you have not cognitively defined it before as "giraffe", you will wonder what it is, and most likely seek a definition for it.

Now this "energy of giraffe" and "actuality of giraffe" can *be* differently in perception based upon your past subconscious and conscious experiences with "energy of giraffe", and the cognitive ideas you have about giraffes in general. This interplay of subconscious, conscious, and cognitive perception now becomes extremely interesting and complex.

Suppose that as a child, you visited the zoo, and you were bitten on the cheek by an angry, aggressive giraffe. As the "energy of giraffe" traveled through your subconscious perceptive systems, it carried with it the energy of "fear and pain". In that moment when "energy of giraffe" bit you, the subconscious thus conscious perceptive identity of "energy of giraffe" was altered. "Energy of giraffe" now subconsciously and consciously also means "fear and pain". Your cognitive mind now decides that the "energy of giraffe" is not only giraffe. Giraffes are scary creatures that bite and cause pain.

Years later, you make a trip to the zoo with your child. He cannot wait to pet the giraffes. Although you have learned through the years that giraffes are almost always gentle and kind, you feel a bit apprehensive. As you approach the giraffe petting station, your child giggles in excitement while your palms sweat and your heart races with fear. You keep telling yourself that "giraffes" are friendly, and watch your child protectively as he begins to stroke one of the "gentle and beautiful" long necked creatures.

You decide in the next moment to push past your ridiculous perception of these gentle beasts. You look your gentle "giraffe" directly in the eyes and reach up to pet it. Just as your hand contacts it fur, it lets out an incredible sneeze. Its head flies towards you. You scream. Your hand flies to your face as you jump back in fear. Your child laughs and says, "You're scared of giraffes! He won't hurt you! He just sneezed!"

You smile at yourself in amusement and frustration. Even your child can perceive your fear. This is much more "giraffe" than you thought it would be. You take a deep breath and soulfully decide to release from fear. You breathe into the expansive possibility that giraffes are really gentle and awesome. You exhale, focus, and soulfully intend to release the fear from your body and mind. In a moment or year you soulfully *be* and know that giraffes are gentle beautiful creatures, and you pet them often. You have transformed your perceptive *being* and perception itself.

As much as you had cognitively decided to change your perception of "giraffe", you could not "make it happen" by the will of your mind. This perception ran much deeper than you thought. You had to feel it and be in it differently. The past "energy of giraffe" deeply embedded in your subconscious nervous and energetic perception had disallowed the possibility of transformation in your perceptive *being*. Your subconscious feeling and knowing were causal. Ultimately, perceptive transformation could only to occur from the inside out.

As humans *being*, we all perceive and live through our "perceptive giraffes." Most often, our perceptions run much deeper than we "think" they do. As we clear our energetic systems through the power of our soulful intention and breath, we allow ourselves to *be* in and perceive transformative change. When we are *being* in this expandable perceptive awareness, our thoughts and actions align with our soulful intention. Through perceptive *being*, we become aware of the causality of our subconscious and conscious perception. Our perception becomes the infinitely expandable sea of possibilities. We perceive truth, become truth, *be* truth, and are causal of it.

*So take a moment or year to notice your perceptive being.*

Do you cling desperately to your thoughts and ideas?

Are you perceptions in line with the being and feeling in your physical body?

Do your cognitive thoughts and actions support your soulful intentions?

How do you perceive your causality in the world?

Are you self- responsible?

Do you "think" one thing but do or *be* another?

Do you solve "problems" through your "thinking" or through your *being*?

Are you often feeling and acting overwhelmed?

Are your perceptions expandable or fixed?

Do you feel and know *and be* that anything is possible, or just "think" that it is?

Do you experience frequent headaches or T.M.J.?

Do you love to be "right"?

# Transformation

When we exist in the reality of transformative *being*, all that we manifest is soulful choice.  As we release from fear, judgment, and pollution in our breath, physical bodies and perceptions, we manifest soulful truth and intention through ourselves and out into the world. We become soulful transformation and expand from and into it. By the smallest shift in our individual *being*, we re-create the fascia of our perceived reality, and thus the reality of the world at large.

**10**

# Wheel Of Life

*"Eleph-ant winked his blind eye, curled his trunk into an antenna, and took three heavy steps to the side. He smiled and tilted his head upward.*
*Baby Ant flew off Eleph-ant's head into the air. His antennae wrapped into a giant ear.*
*'Oh Eleph-ant!' he cried out in amazement! ' I can hear the jungle!'*
*Mama Ant saw the sky."*

The wheel of life spins infinitely as it moves in us, through us and around us.  As the sea of possibility endlessly expands and collapses in transformation, we draw from it the soulful inspiration that spins our reality and molds destiny. Miraculously we exist, humans *being* suspended on a spinning world, microcosms of universal energy. With every breath we take we expand possibility and collapse into choice; releasing our soulful intentions in and through us, as we manifest the energy of our *being* out into the world that we spin… This is our journey through the wheel of life.

Expansion-Intention-Manifestation of Energy-into Being: Constant instantaneous transformation from the inside out: from the sea of infinite possibility through the soul, the physical body, the perceptive sense, and out into transformative reality. In every less than a second, we create and recreate the wheel. I and We choose what, how and why we spin.

As we travel through the Wheel of Life from the inside out, we unravel our transformative process. We gain access and insight into our transformative pathways. We become aware of the energetic threads that freely spin us, and those that bind and tangle manifestation of desired choice. We open into the infinite question of our *being*; constant instantaneous transformation.

# Dianna

I will never forget that morning. I was about ten weeks pregnant with my daughter, and pretty much sick and tired of everything from the moment I was awakened by the deafening screech of my alarm. Literally quite ill, I somehow made a cup of herbal tea, squeezed my thickening body into a pair of yoga pants, and in an hour's time found myself unlocking the yoga studio door.

My key stuck a bit in the lock. I so didn't want to be here. My true desire was to be in bed with the covers pulled over my head for at least another six hours. I paused a moment to fight off the queasiness, and then rattled the key in the lock until the stubborn door finally opened. "Maybe it will be a small class today", I thought to myself hopefully as I unrolled my mat and hid my "anti puke" crackers underneath the right-hand corner. In an attempt to change my attitude, I settled into child's pose and took a deep breath. Just then I heard voices from the hall. Frustrated, I heaved my heavy body up from the floor, sighed, and did my best to be in kind thoughts and don my loving yoga teacher smile.

And then they came in, all of them, a larger class than I had seen in months. I tried my best not to vomit, and smiled at each one of them graciously as I signed them in. There was a broad range of them indeed. As I sent them to their mats I analyzed the situation: five agro athletes, four complete novices, six seasoned practitioners, two totally stiff guys, the girl with a bad wrist, the guy with inexplicable low back pain, and three of my private therapeutic clients with ailments consisting of a herniated disc, a recovering rotator cuff, and a hip replacement. Now this would be an interesting crew. I fought the urge to cry.

"Why", I thought to myself, "must they all show up for class today, of all days? Why does this never happen on the mornings when I am wide awake, ready to teach, and overflowing with brilliant creative yogic thoughts, anatomical prowess, and words of wisdom? Why today?"

Mats unrolled, the endless mass of students sat in silence, patiently waiting to begin their practice. I took another deep breath and attempted to center myself.

Just as I was going to wade through the maze of mats to the front of the room, I saw a shadow outside the studio door. "Great! Another late student!" For a split second, I contemplated locking the latecomer out; after all, it was far past the beginning of class time, and all I really wanted to do in the moment was get to the crackers that lay underneath the corner of my mat. I was just thinking this was probably not the kindest thought, when the door opened and in she walked. Dianna! I had not seen her for about six months. She radiated a glowing apologetic inquisitive smile, and I immediately waved her to unroll her mat in the last available space. Dianna was one of a kind.

I first met her three years or so after she was diagnosed with a rare form of leukemia. She had attended my class a few times, and then asked me if I would mind doing a few private sessions with herself and her family. I didn't know she was seriously ill until she told me in her first private session. I had noticed before that she was maybe a bit thin and frail, but that is not such an uncommon thing for Scandinavian women in their late fifties or early sixties. In fact, she always had quite a glow about her that radiated healthy energy and timeless beauty. She never seemed like she was sick or in pain, and she certainly didn't act like it. She smiled and radiated grace from her *being* where ever she went.

According to Dianna, she had not always been that way. In the prime of her life, she had been a highly successful, completely stressed out real estate agent, who in her words was "somewhat of a materialistic, self centered bitch". She was controlling, physically held, and highly driven. Apparently, by the time I met her, she had been so beaten down by her disease that she had relinquished all control over herself and her world, and chosen to lead a life of born of love and inquisition. Sometimes, during a session with her, I would notice the residual held energy in her jaw or hands, but for the most part, it was hard to imagine that the open gracious *being* before me had ever been anything but that. The mere presence of Dianna seemed to make everyone's day a little brighter.

Momentarily, wrapped in the warmth of her smile, I found my way to the front of the room, greeted my students, and began facilitating meditation. I sighed, grabbed for one of my crackers, and quietly walked over to Dianna's mat. In a whisper, I asked her how she was feeling. "I'm fine", she replied. "Maybe be a little careful of pressing on my low back. I just had three chemo shots there a couple of days ago. I *am* feeling a bit tired because I walked the Ten K Walk for Breast Cancer yesterday, but no worries. Thanks for asking."

I stood there, immobilized, suddenly sick with horror. My words stuck in my throat. "Good to see you", I finally choked out, as I felt the tears well up behind my eyes. Here *I* was, feeling sorry for myself because I had the blessing of being sick with the gift of a child, the gift the beautiful students that lay before me, and the unprecedented freedom opportunity to teach and learn from them. Here *I* stood, in this moment, a healthy human *being* in complete lack of gratitude for the miracle of my life and the life I was creating; while right next to me, head bowed humbly in child's pose, was a human being in the depths of suffering and the brink of death ever so graciously gifting *me* with her radiant *being* and positive energy, and all the while thanking me for my half present angry *being*.

I am not sure how long I stood there frozen, appalled by my own lack of awareness, staring down at the beauty of the *being* that lay before me. I was in the presence of transformative grace. Dianna had the ability to be in complete awareness of the precariousness of her physical body and reality, yet all the while, be so undeniably confident in her place in the universe and her soulful purpose that she radiated sheer bliss through the decaying container of her human. She had not only perfected the art of how to *be* in *being*. Dianna understood what her *being* meant in the universe. She embodied pure soulfully chosen transformation. She was free from the prison of ego and self. She *was* transformative choice.

I however, clearly remained behind bars. Now, painfully aware of this, thanks to Dianna, I somehow continued on despite my ungraciousness and lack of self-awareness, and managed to facilitate class. I don't remember much of what I said or taught that day. What I do remember is studying the *being* of Dianna the entire time, and noticing how she smiled and beamed with joy while the agro-athletes complained about their tired muscles, the therapeutic cases winced in frustration, and the novice and advanced practitioners attempted to disentangle from their egos. She moved the power of the universe through the shell of her human in complete effortlessness. At the brink of death, Dianna was more alive than any *being* in the room, myself included.

I never saw her again after that day. I wish that I could have, I would have thanked her. It has been a few years now since Dianna passed from the physical world, yet I still think of her often and wonder…

"Must we, as humans *being*, be on the verge of death before we can truly appreciate the beauty and opportunity of every less than a second of our lives? Must we be in the end of our life cycle to confidently *be* in gratitude for the moment and understand our timeless purpose in the ever- expanding universe? Can we choose to move through the less than a second cycle of our expansion, intention, manifestation of energy into *being* in constant transformative expansion because we *choose* to, and not because we *have* to? Can we *be* the question and the answer in simultaneity as we travel through the wheel of life?

# LIFEYOGA Wheel Of Life

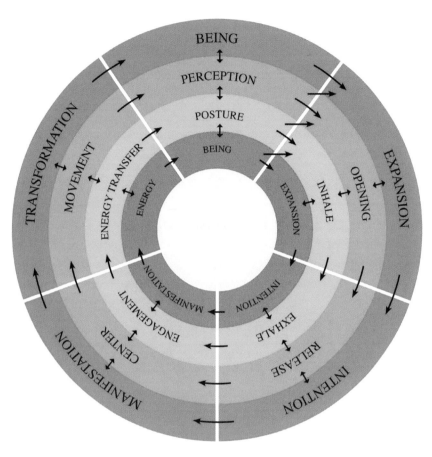

■ SOUL
■ BODY
■ PERCEPTION
■ TRANSFORMATION

# The Tool

The **Wheel Of Life** visual tool allows us to travel from universal possibility, through the soul, the physical body and world, and out into transformative collective consciousness. Our experiential journey leads us to expand our perceptions of "how I am", "how the world is", and "what is possible". The avenues of the Wheel of Life are multidimensional. The endless ways of connecting and moving through this visual transformative process allow us to see and experience the blocks and barriers that prevent soulful transformation, and discover new pathways of *being* that support and manifest desired change.

The **Wheel Of Life** can be and has been used in various applications. Originally developed as a tool for the LIFEYOGA teacher training to aid teacher-training candidates in the understanding of LIFEYOGA philosophy, anatomical energetic analysis, and expansive thought and decision making, the **Wheel of Life** has also proved to be greatly beneficial in many facets of life education. Thus far, it has been successful as an aid in the discovery of personal transformation, health and wellness, business, and a plethora of educational trainings.

The **Wheel Of Life** has been utilized by physicians, therapists, chiropractors and body workers as a diagnostic tool, as well as a means to gain insight and understanding of the connections between the soul, the mind, and the nervous system as they relate to the manifestations and cures of pain and disease. It has also been used in the areas of health and wellness as a pathway to integrate and unify the ideologies of eastern and western medicines.

This tool has been effective for corporate brainstorming and the development of business strategies. It offers the business and entrepreneurial worlds a transformative pathway that creates a framework for the opportunity to expand upon present ideas, and create new and ingenious ways to soulfully manifest abundance in the world.

The following pages provide an inside out transformational journey through the **Wheel of Life**. This adventure begins in the endless sea of possibility, travels through the soul, body, and perception out to the realm of causal transformative *being*. The process of this expedition breaks down in detail the causal energy of transformative process, and offers the reader an opportunity to self reflect and notice his or her personal process of *being*.

# Possibility

The sea of possibilities is the endless universal energy of instantaneous transformation. Infinite and sometimes seemingly intangible, universal energy, or that which simply *is*, is always available to us. It is only our human *being* that limits our access to this transformative power.

Whether defined as "collective consciousness", "God", or "Cosmic Soup", *it* is causal of our reality as we move *it* through our *being* in conscious or subconscious soulful intention. *It* is all we are from, all that we are, and all that we create. *It is.*

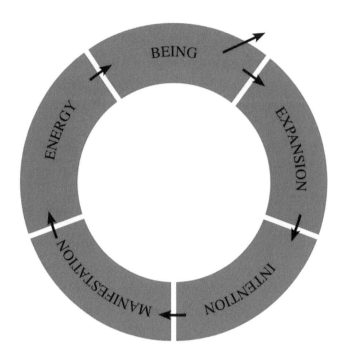

# The Soul

The soul is forever swimming through the vast sea of possibilities, choosing in every less than a second the transformation we experience. The soulful sense is the beginning of our journey through the wheel of life. It is the root source of our *being*, the foundation that creates our soulful intention and causes our transformative reality. How we are *being* in our soulful sense is ultimately causal of our existence.

*EXPANSION:* However the soul is *being* in expansion, how subconscious feeling and knowing are able to open into and access the sea of possibility determines our transformative choice. Our soulful expansion dictates the possibility of what soulful intentions are available to us.

*INTENTION:* From our soulful expansion, we choose our intention. Our ability to soulfully choose possibility, shed all conflicting possibilities, and release into the intention of choice determines our ability to clearly *be* in soulful intention. Subconsciously/sometimes consciously, however and whatever we intend, is the choice from which we manifest.

*MANIFESTATION:* Soulful manifestation determines how we engage in and manifest chosen intention. Our ability to soulfully manifest determines the power and type of intentional energy released in manifestation.

*ENERGY:* Soulful energy is the result of soulful manifestation of intention. It is the raw power that spins us. It is the energy of our soulful *being*.

*BEING:* Our soulful state if *being* is the result of the soulful energy we create. Soulful *being* dictates soulful expansion. Our soulful *being* is causal in the physical body and physical world. It is our connection between the spiritual realm and the physical reality.

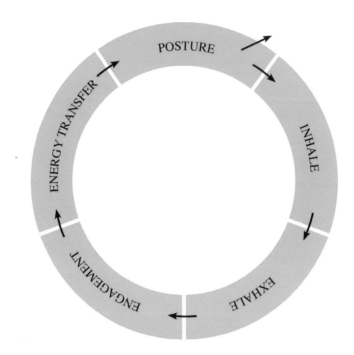

# The Body

The physical body is the physical world manifestation of soulful energy. Our human bodies are our tools; the means by which we expand, release, and manifest our soulful energy into physical actualization. Through the breath, our physical bodies become the causal physical energy that creates and manifests our physical reality. Transformative soulful intention must move freely through the breath and our physical *being* to create soulfully desired transformative reality. How we are *being* in our physical bodies is causal in all transformation of our physical body, life, and world.

*INHALE:* Expansion correlates to inhalation in the physical body. As we breathe in, we open the nervous system to the possibility of manifesting soulful intention through the human body. Inhalation is causal of exhalation.

*EXHALE:* Intention correlates to exhalation in the physical body. In exhalation, we release and clear the nervous system, allowing soulful intention to release into the body. The release of exhalation dictates if, how, and what soulful intention manifests and moves through the body.

*ENGAGEMENT:* Manifestation correlates to engagement in the physical body. However we engage intention in the breath, nervous system, and physical body determines what and how we manifest. Whatever and however we manifest is causal of the type and amount of energy we release through the body.

*ENERGY TRANSFER:* Energy correlates to energy transfer in the physical body. The energy released from engagement in manifestation must travel through the human body to create change. The way in which we transfer manifested energy of soulful intention through both our physical and psycho-energetic systems is causal of our posture in the physical world.

*POSTURE:* Physical *being* is the physical manifestation of soulful *being*. Posture, or the *physical energetic state of being* is, in every less than a second, the result of the expansion of the inhale, the release of the exhale, engagement in the physical body, and the transfer of manifested energy through the energetic systems. Our physical posture or state of *being* determines the expansion of the following inhalation. Posture in the physical body is causal of perception.

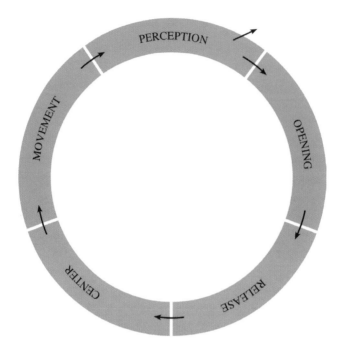

# Perception

In every less than a second, as soulful intention becomes embodied by the physical *being*, the perceptive sense subconsciously/ sometimes consciously tells us " if and how soulful intention is moving through us " and "what is possible" in the next breath. Our *posture*, or physical state of *being* is our lens of perception. We can only perceive from where and what we are. We perceive from how we are *being* in the breath, the subconscious/sometimes conscious nervous system, and body. How we are *being* in perception is causal of all cognitive thought, action, and transformative opportunity. Our perceptions mold our reality.

*OPENING:* Expansion correlates to opening in the perceptive sense. However we are *being in posture* in the physical body and nervous system dictates how open we feel and our perceptive possibility for expansion and choice. Our perception and feeling of opening dictates our perception of release.

*RELEASE:* Intention correlates to release in the perceptive sense. However we expand in inhalation and release into intention in exhalation in the physical body and nervous system determines our subconscious/ sometimes conscious perception of release. Our perception and feeling of release determines our perception of center.

*CENTER:* Manifestation correlates to center in the perceptive sense. Our subconscious/sometimes conscious perception of release and engagement into center determines how centered we feel. However we are released and engaged in the breath, physical body and nervous system determines our perception of center and our ability to manifest from center. Our perception and feeling of center dictate how we perceive movement of manifested energy.

*MOVEMENT:* Energy correlates to movement in the perceptive sense. As energy travels through the physical and psycho-energetic systems, we subconsciously/sometimes consciously perceive movement or change from the basis of our perceptive center. However we perceive and feel this movement or change in energy is causal of how we are *being* in perception.

*PERCEPTION: Being* correlates to perception. How we are subconsciously/ sometimes consciously being in perception is the result of how we perceive *opening, release, center,* and *movement* of energetic soulful intention through our human *being.* This ultimate perception of *feeling and being* is causal of cognitive thought and action, and determines our ability to access the transformative sea of possibilities. How we are *being* perceptively, subconsciously/sometimes consciously, is causal of how we expand into and create the transformative realities of our bodies, our lives, and our world.

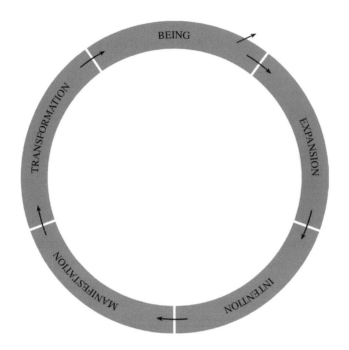

# Transformation

As humans being we exist in a constant state of instantaneous transformation. By simply existing, through the transformation of our energy, we are constantly transforming our own *being* and our world. This ultimate causal energy of our *being*, our *transformative being*, is, in every less than a second, released from our soulful bodies out into the endless sea of possibilities. Our *transformative being* causes our reality.

*EXPANSION:* Expansion correlates to transformative expansion. However our human *being opens in expansion through the soul, body, and perception* creates the energy of our expansive transformative *being*. This energy of *being* transformative expansion determines the possibilities of our transformative reality. Transformative expansion is causal of transformative intention.

*INTENTION:* Intention correlates to transformative intention. However our human *being chooses* soulful intention, releases into chosen intention, and manifests it through the body and perceptive sense determines the transformative intention of our *being*. This energy of *being transformative soulful intention* is the causal intention of our transformative reality. Transformative intention is causal of transformative manifestation.

*MANIFESTATION:* Manifestation correlates to transformative manifestation. However soulful intention engages in manifestation and releases physical and psycho-energetic energy through the body and perceptive sense determines our transformative power to manifest, and what we manifest through our *being*. This energy of *being transformative manifestation* causes the manifestation of our transformative reality. Transformative manifestation is causal of transformative energy.

*TRANSFORMATION:* Energy correlates to transformation. However manifested soulful energy moves through the physical body and perceptive sense determines the transformative energy of our *being*. This *being transformative energy* is causal of transformative being.

*BEING: Being* correlates to *transformative being*. Ultimately, however and whatever soulful intention travels through the breath, physical body and perceptive sense determines our *transformative being*. *Transformative being* is the result of our less than a second journey through *expansion, intention, manifestation, and energy. Transformative being* is the causal energy that chooses our transformative reality and sea of possibility.

# Transformative Choice

The transformative reality that *I* and *we* create greatly influences our ability to access the sea of possibilities. Our state of individual and collective transformative *being*, and how we *are being* in transformative process, decide what is possible choice in the realm of infinite possibilities.

*Transformative being* becomes *transformative choice* when through our *being we choose* to exist in the reality of transformative awareness and soulful intention. If we choose, in awareness, breath by breath, to expand into our soulful sense, release into our chosen soulful intention, manifest this intention freely from the core of our being through the physical body and out into the world; we are *being chosen transformation*. Through this *being*, with every breath, we endlessly expand and consciously instantaneously choose our reality.

Every less than a second, we breathe, we choose, we engage, we spin, transform and collapse back into the center of the wheel. We endlessly become from our journey's infinite end. The answer asks the question.

# 11

# If

On a silent distant shore, surf rumbles endlessly. Humans *being*.

In that less than a second, they sit huddled in the corner of a cardboard box holding their ears from the blast of shrapnel while a random band plays, and thousands of deaf eared fans scream out loud and dance to the latest beat. Humans *being*.

In rolls the tide. Somewhere, the party is over. He sips his morning coffee as he buries last night's party trash on the beach and smiles up at his beautiful daughter. She chokes a kiss upon his balmy weathered forehead, and leaves for school to study environmental science. Humans *being*.

Waves swell into random moments. Someplace, a lonely child cries with starvation as a surgeon staples the stomach of a famous rock star before she dies of obesity. Humans *being*.

Waves break. Surgery somehow sewn up, celebrity life saved, he steps outside for a smoke and feeds the cancer that silently kills him. He crushes his cigarette butt into the tired old sand, hops into his shiny new sports car, and heads out to a world hunger benefit dinner. Humans *being*.

Surf sprays. Here, in a five star seaside hotel, the party begins. Bellies full of rich food and good intention, doctors dance in a smoke filled room to the deafening rhythm of shrapnel as it ricochets from the walls of a cardboard box constructed from a rain forest. Humans *being*.

The tide recedes. She walks home from school, picks up a swollen cigarette butt from the shifting sand, and wonders if any of it matters. Her father waits with open arms. She offers up a hungry smile to him as salty balmy droplets stream down her face. He holds her ears in his hands and dreams that he can save her from this undertow of tears. She wishes she could fly.

*What if* she *would* fly? *What if* every human *being* soulfully believed in flight? *What if* all humans *being* found their voices and chose to sing from the soul? *What if* all humans *would be* in release from suffering and ignorance and manifest love and awareness through their *being*? *What if* every human could be the energy of chosen soulful intention? *What if I and we would* consciously breathe the unfolding of humanity as it collapses into reality? *What if?*

*And If* you ever feel for a moment that what you feel doesn't matter…as a human *being*… it does.

*If* you ever breathe for a moment, and that breath doesn't matter…as a human *being*… it does.

*If* you ever think for a moment that what you think doesn't matter…as a human *being*…. it does.

*If* you ever *be* for a moment…and it matters or doesn't matter…***IT IS.***

Made in the USA
Lexington, KY
20 May 2014